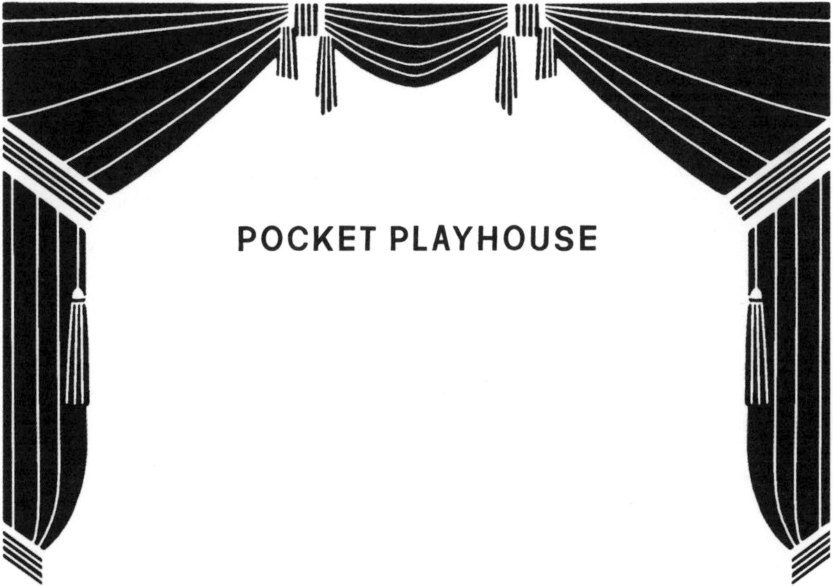

POCKET PLAYHOUSE

by the same author

FICTION
The Tin Men
The Russian Interpreter
Towards the End of the
Morning
A Very Private Life
Sweet Dreams
The Trick of It
A Landing on the Sun
Now You Know
Headlong
Spies
Skios

NON-FICTION
Constructions
Celia's Secret: an investigation
(with David Burke)
The Human Touch
Collected Columns
Stage Directions
My Father's Fortune

PLAYS
The Two of Us
Alphabetical Order
Donkeys' Years
Clouds
Balmoral
Make and Break
Noises Off
Benefactors
Look Look
Here
Now You Know
Copenhagen
Alarms & Excursions
Democracy
Afterlife
Matchbox Theatre

FILM AND TELEVISION
Clockwise
First and Last
Remember Me?

TRANSLATIONS
The Seagull (Chekhov)
Uncle Vanya (Chekhov)
Three Sisters (Chekhov)
The Cherry Orchard (Chekhov)
The Sneeze (Chekhov)
Wild Honey (Chekhov)
The Fruits of Enlightenment
(Tolstoy)
Exchange (Trifonov)
Number One (Anouilh)

POCKET
PLAYHOUSE

Thirty-Six Short Entertainments by
MICHAEL FRAYN

ff

First published in 2017
by Faber & Faber Ltd,
Bloomsbury House,
74–77 Great Russell Street, London WC1B 3DA

Typeset by Faber & Faber Ltd
Printed and bound in Europe

The right of Michael Frayn to be identified as author of this work
has been asserted in accordance with Section 77 of the
Copyright, Designs and Patents Act 1988

A CIP record for this book
is available from the British Library

ISBN 978–0–571–33315–8

2 4 6 8 10 9 7 5 3 1

INSTRUCTIONS FOR ASSEMBLING YOUR POCKET PLAYHOUSE

You will need:

A sharp knife

Glue

Complete sobriety, dedication, and commitment

Planning permission

Heritage Lottery Fund grant

Potential patrons of high net worth wearing black tie, together with prosecco, canapés, waiters, security staff, and charity auctioneer

Assembly

Soak the potential patrons of high net worth **PPHNW** in the prosecco **P** and with the help of the charity auctioneer **CA** carefully separate from **£££**.

While **PPHNW** are marinating, fold the planning permission **PP** along the dotted line **DL**, and insert the tabs **T2** . . . **Tx** into the slots **S4** . . . **Qj**. Using the glue **G**, stick **sine K3** to **cosine C4**, being careful not to confuse **K** with K, or k with **k**.

Now install the fully automated lighting and air-conditioning system **FALACS** (not included), and bend sideways to look backwards while still being certain to face forwards.

You can't do it . . . ?

No, of course not. This is because you have stuck the flap **Z** to the coefficient of **D**, which is not what you were told to do.

So unglue it again . . . Unglue it . . .

Come on, we haven't got all night . . .

No luck . . . ?

Oh, dear. You weren't using Superglue, were you . . . ?

You were. Of course. So now both the flap **Z** and the coefficient of **D** are stuck to your fingers **FF**. Also to your sleeve **S** and the cup of cold coffee **CC** left over from breakfast **B**.

So this is when you will need the sharp knife **K**. Which is where . . . ?

You can't find it. You know you put it down somewhere . . . In the old teapot **TP**, perhaps, where you keep the various 10-per-cent-off vouchers you always forget to use . . . ?

No, no, no – I was making a little joke **J** . . .

Oh, good, you've found **K**. And where was it, as a matter of interest . . . ?

Right in front of your eyes **EE**. Exactly where you put it. Of course.

So now, with a quick stabbing movement of the knife **K** . . .

Oh no! Oh, for heaven's sake!

Yes, but stop shouting and waving hand **H** about! Wound **W** is surely not life-threatening, and you're getting blood **B** everywhere . . . !

Keep calm! Simply apply the plaster **P** to **W** . . .

P, P, P! P to W!

[4]

I'm *not* shouting . . . !

All right, then – just chuck the whole thing into **WPB** and go to **A & E** . . .

THE HERITAGE EXPERIENCE

Welcome aboard the London Heritage Experience, the tour that makes London's history more historical than ever before!

We kick off in Piccadilly Circus, famous as the Heart of the Empire, though the Empire itself is now situated a few hundred yards away in Leicester Square (five screens, twenty screenings daily). The statue of Eros in the centre of the Circus takes its name from the courageous Cockneys celebrated in so many films about the Second World War.

Coming up on our right – Buckingham Palace, home of Britain's world-famous Royal Family. The building is not the Elizabethan original, now in Texas, but an exact reconstruction made out of fibreglass by technicians from BBC TV's historical reconstruction department, as are all the members of the family who appear on the balcony in front of it at times of national rejoicing. The originals have been removed to a former

World War II air-raid shelter adjoining Clapham South underground station for safekeeping.

> *Fact*: Britain produces more kings and queens than the rest of Europe put together. If you include princes and princesses, royal dukes and duchesses, and illegitimate but ennobled offspring, their accumulated tonnage exceeds that of Holland's annual potato crop.

We are now passing through Pall Mall, notorious for the so-called gentlemen's clubs that have proliferated in the area. The frontages are carefully anonymous, the drinks pricey, and the girls in very short supply. Tourists beware! Hands on your wallets!

On our left, the Houses of Parliament. 'Big Ben' is not the name of the tower, as most people believe – it's the man who sells T-shirts on the stand outside. The clocktower itself is actually called Tiny Tim, and figures in TV adaptations of Dickens's much-loved classic *Little Nell*. It's interesting to note that most Members of Parliament have been convicted of offences of one sort or another, and attend the House on day release as part of an imaginative back-to-work scheme . . .

We are now entering the City, once world-famous as 'the Square Mile', now, thanks to a notorious ruling by the European Court, 'the 2.59 Square Kilometres'. The hedge fund analysts and arbitrageurs you can see on their way to the local champagne bars are all played by out-of-work actors, or students doing work experience. The originals are in the Cayman Islands and elsewhere, enjoying their tax breaks and bonuses. Unless they're in Zurich or New York, outraged that their bonuses are a few million pounds smaller than they surely have every right to expect.

On your left, St Paul's Cathedral, one of the City's famous churches, which include St John's, St George's, and St Ringo's. A story whispered in the Cathedral's Whispering Gallery will pass all the way round the dome, then through the Palace of Westminster, the clubs of St James's and the champagne bars of the City, to end up on the front page of the following day's *Daily Mail* . . .

Eyes right! – the Tower of London. Known by irreverent Londoners as 'the bloody Tower,' like all the other bloody towers on the London skyline. Originally planned to be fifty storeys high and shaped like a flattened beer-can, it fell foul of unimaginative early planning legislation. So many actresses playing Anne Boleyn have had their heads cut off here that if they were all piled on top of each other it would put the present building back in contention with the Gherkin and the Shard.

>   *Fact*: The famous Beefeaters guarding the Tower no longer eat beef! They were switched to a low-cholesterol vegetarian diet after the recent horse-meat scandal.

We're now passing Madame Tussaud's. Many of the famous waxwork figures in here have been sold to collectors in America and replaced by the actual celebrities they represent, who are less likely to melt as a result of global warming, and who can in any case be more cheaply replaced.

If you look out to the left you can see . . . nothing, really, just at the moment, thanks to the traffic congestion! This is a reconstruction of what Lord Nelson could see when he famously put his blind eye to the telescope. A more-than-life-size fibreglass model of the original telescope forms the column on which his statue stands in Trafalgar Square.

Eyes shut, please, to avoid seeing the sheer ordinariness of the next few streets, which are still waiting to have some historical significance discovered, and suitable heritage sites constructed . . .

Eyes open again! On your right is a typical English pub, the Ritz. If it hasn't yet been the setting of a long-running TV series it soon will be. The name comes from the many writs for libel, breach of copyright, and inappropriate sexual behaviour that the series will give rise to.

> *Fact*: The word pub is short for public convenience. Public conveniences were the forerunners of the modern convenience store.

The historic public conveniences on the left now house the National Museum of Public Convenience. They were used in the shooting of Jane Austen's *Wuthering Heights* as the location of Nell Gwynne's house . . . The costumes for the production cost £273,000.

On the right . . . *Right*, please, ladies and gentlemen! Not left! No looking left! The tableau on the left of police beating up demonstrators is merely part of reality, not of our national heritage! In any case the demonstrators are all really undercover policemen.

So, yes, thank you – on the right is the Royal Exchange, where Henry VIII used to swap his wives. If fibreglass could speak what a story it could tell for modern scriptwriters to improve upon!

Eyes left again, please! The scene on the right of people queuing for food handouts is merely part of a TV documentary, and entirely fictitious!

Fact: Queen Victoria took her title not from Victoria Station, as most people believe, but from the Queen Victoria pub in the Mile End Road, one of the so-called Inns of Court. She later married the landlord, Albert Hall, the youngest of the Five Singing Music Halls.

On your right is Ye Olde Curiosity Shoppe, the setting for a famous TV documentary about the killing of unwanted cats.

Westminster Abbey, on your left, has been used as the setting for many TV spectaculars about the Royal Family. Visitors sometimes ask why the knave of the cathedral is so called. The name derives from the tomb of the Black Prince, otherwise known as the Knave of Spades. It has a famous echo. I'll demonstrate. 'Hello!' Now – listen . . .

– 'Hello! All our echoes are busy at the moment, but your call is important to us, and has been placed in a queue. It will be echoed as soon as possible.'

That's all, folks! Hope you enjoyed the London Experience, the experience that enables you to experience the experience of actual experience! As you leave, notice the figure of a man by the door holding his hand out. This is not, as many people believe, a statue of Oliver Twist asking for more – it's the real-life me, awaiting your kind appreciation.

SO WHO IS SYLVIA?

Darling, you remember Sylvia?

– Sylvia? Who's Sylvia?

What do you mean, 'Who's Sylvia?' That woman with the surname we can never remember. Anyway, I ran into Mildred today . . .

– You ran into *Mildred*?

Mildred, yes. Anyway, guess what . . .

– Hold on. It wasn't Sylvia you ran into?

Sylvia? No – Mildred, Mildred! Why should I have run into Sylvia?

– Because you said did I remember Sylvia. But it was *Mildred* you ran into?

Mildred! Yes!

– Mildred. Right.

And don't start saying 'Who's Mildred?' You know perfectly well who Mildred is. Mildred and Charlie! The Swains!

– The Swains? What, those friends of whoever it is?

Not *their* Swains! *Our* Swains! The couple who've had that great falling-out with the woman who used to be married to Jeremy someone.

– *Jeremy* someone? I thought he was called *Simon* someone?

Simon someone? You're thinking of that man we met in Italy somewhere whose *brother* was called Simon, and he had some kind of thing with the wife of that man in the Department of whatever it was . . .

– *Simon* did?

Simon? Not *Simon*! The man whose *brother's* called Simon! And whose cousin, incidentally, lives in the same street as her.

– As Sylvia?

Darling, try not to be any stupider than God made you. The same street as Mildred! Don't you listen to anything I say? Anyway, guess what . . .

– She's dead.

Dead? Who's dead?

– Mildred.

Mildred? Dead?

– Or Sylvia.

Sylvia? Why should Sylvia be dead?

– Yellow fever? Boredom?

Sylvia's not dead!

– Oh, good. I thought that's what all this was leading up to. 'You know Sylvia? Et cetera, et cetera. Et cetera, et cetera. Well . . . (*Dramatic pause*) . . . she's dead!' But she's *not* dead? Sylvia?

Of course she's not dead! In fact she and the Swains found themselves staying in the same hotel on holiday. That's what I was going to tell you!

– Which Swains are we talking about now? Our Swains or the other ones?

Our Swains! Apparently she adores them. And all our Swains adore her!

A KNIGHT TO REMEMBER

Thank you so much, Your Majesty! A knighthood! It's what I've always wanted!

I know you've got a lot of other people to knight this morning, and I don't want to hold you up, but I do just want to tell you how really chuffed I am. Last year you knighted my old friend Bungo Woolenough – or Sir Benedict Woolenough, as you probably know him! – and when I had lunch with him the following week and the maître d' said 'This way, if you please, Sir Benedict,' I thought, 'Yes! I want one of those, please!'

I just can't wait to phone him! 'Bungo? It's me . . . ! No, *not* Cheesy! Sir Charles, if you please! Sir Charles Chedworth!'

It's as good as a tonic! I feel like a new man!

Though what I've done to deserve such a wonderful honour I really don't know! 'Services to business and international relations' – oh, come on! I just did my bit to keep the UK tax avoidance industry on its feet. And, all right, yes – I helped out in my spare time with charitable work for distressed investors in the Cayman Islands. And if I only got paid a few measly millions for my efforts, who cares – I loved the work!

Anyway, if I may say so, Your Majesty, you performed the ceremony really beautifully! That sword of yours looks awfully sharp and I was just a little bit nervous that you might come down slightly off-centre and take a piece out of my ear! We're none of us as young as we were! I know that if I'd been the one waving the sword about I might well have put Your Majesty's eye out! So, well done, Your Majesty!

And I just love your palace . . . ! Hold on a moment, though – someone tugging at my sleeve . . .

You're what . . . ? An equerry . . . ? Nice to meet you! I'm Charles. Or rather *Sir* Charles! I haven't got used to it yet . . . ! And you're . . . ? Lieutenant Colonel Sir James Trouser? So – Jim, then, if I may, as one knight to another . . . ! Her Majesty's got other people to knight? I know she has! But, Jim, I'm sure we were both brought up always to say thank you to our hostess!

Where was I, Your Majesty? Oh, yes, your palace! You've done it up really beautifully! Such tasteful furnishings! And paintings by some really top-class artists that even *I've* heard of!

Oh, and your crown! It goes so well with your dress!

I'm coming, Jim, I'm coming . . . So, Your Majesty, thank you for everything. The canapés were delicious! Did you make them yourself . . . ? No, of course not. Well, then, you must let me know the name of your caterers!

I have to go, Your Majesty. Apparently. Your friend Jim here is being very pressing . . . I'm sure that Bungo – Sir Benedict – would have sent his love if he'd known I was going to be seeing you . . .

All right, Jim, take it easy – no need to twist my arm behind my back . . . So give me a call, Your Majesty, when you're a bit less busy, and come and see us. Edna – Lady Chedworth! – is dying to meet you, so bring the Duke and we can all four of us have a nice relaxed cup of tea together.

I don't think we can promise you any kind of honour, but Lady Chedworth does make a pretty good Victoria sponge!

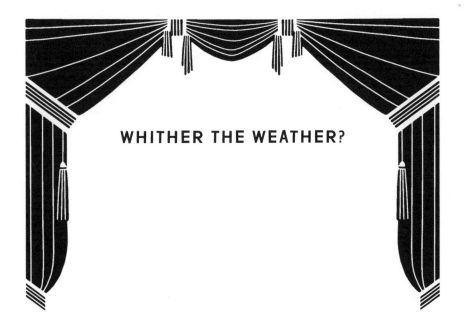

WHITHER THE WEATHER?

Good evening! A funny old day it's been weather-wise today! It started out not funny or old at all, but pretty serious, as days go at this time of year, and surprisingly young. But by the afternoon it was getting noticeably more comic and middle-aged, and by evening it was, well, quite hilariously geriatric.

Tomorrow, I think, we've got some slightly more familiar weather in store for us. A rather misty and murky start in most places, with a chance of spits and spots of rain.

You may be wondering, before we go any further, why mist always comes in association with murk, and murk with mist, and spits with spots, and spots with spits. You can see what's causing it on the satellite picture: it's this binary alliterative system moving in from the Atlantic.

The alliteration is going to deepen as the day goes on, and the system works its way through. The mist is likely to become even murkier, and the murk mistier. Here and there the spits and spots will give way to dibs and dobs and blibs and blobs, with outbreaks of splishes and sploshes on high ground.

In the afternoon we'll see the alliteration gradually clearing from the west. The spits and spots will die away to spotless spits and spitless spots, with a slight possibility of mistless murk and murkless mist. In some districts a few last bits and bobs may persist – with perhaps here and there lingering dribs and drabs, and even, further north, some persistent flibs and flobs and wibs and wobs.

By the weekend, I think, we'll have said goodbye to the alliteration. It's still going to be a little on the binary side, though, with combinations about normal for this time of year: cats and dogs, hail and farewell, sun and heir. In East Anglia and the Lowlands of Scotland there are Met Office warnings of more serious literary devices, so be prepared for synecdoche, and maybe even litotes and hendiadys.

Further south, after all that alliteration, we may at last be enjoying a spot of good old-fashioned end-rhyme. A few flashes and crashes, perhaps, with in places the cats and dogs turning to cats and rats, or even dogs and hogs. For the most part, though, a pretty fair and square weekend.

The long-term forecast: a spell of full-scale prosody, with widespread iambic pentameters, and perhaps here and there some quite unseasonable amphibrachs and dactyls.

>   And whether the weather gets worser or drier,
>   Or hotter or cooler or wetter,

With air-pressures lower or pollen-counts higher,
To have it in dactyls sounds better.

Or these:
Spondees.

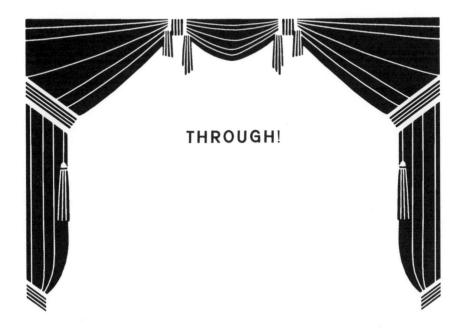

THROUGH!

Hello . . . ? Am I through . . . ? Are you there . . . ?

You are! I don't believe it! Wonderful!

Oh no, oh no, oh curse . . . !

No, sorry – you're *still* there . . . Thank God – I thought you might have rung off again! I dropped the phone . . . ! I was so surprised to hear your voice! *Anyone's* voice . . . !

Yes, because I was fast asleep when you answered! It's that music you play! It's very soporific – it keeps going round in circles! And that voice every few seconds saying 'All our operators are busy.' Like being hypnotised.

I was actually in the middle of a dream. I dreamt I was phoning an emergency line about something, and I was waiting and waiting to get through – and then suddenly there was this voice in my ear, and I woke up with a terrible start, because it *wasn't* a dream! I actually *was* on the phone! I *had* been waiting and waiting to get through! And at last I *had*!

So thank you, thank you!

Only, hold on . . . Who have I got through *to*? I can't remember who I was phoning! Was it the gas? Or was it the electricity? No, I know – it's the phone! The phone's gone wrong again . . .

No, it hasn't. This *is* the phone . . .

I knew perfectly well who I was phoning when I phoned you . . .

No – wait! Please don't hang up! Not after all this!

What was I phoning about? I might remember what I was phoning about if I could remember who I was phoning . . .

A reference number? Yes! Good! I'll give you a reference number! Then we'll know what this is all about. Hold on. I do have a reference number . . . !

I *did* have a reference number . . .

It was written down on the back of the Council Tax thing – where's the Council Tax thing . . . ?

Oh – it isn't the Council Tax I'm calling about, is it? That's not the Council . . . ? No, no – I *don't* want the Council . . . ! Stop, though, wait!

Please don't ring off!

It must have fallen off the table while I was asleep . . . It's probably *under* the table. Only I can't see anything . . . Why can't I see anything? Because it's dark! Why's it dark, though? It wasn't dark when I phoned you . . . What's happened? Has something happened? An eclipse, or a volcano, or something . . . ?

The middle of the night . . . ? It can't be! I haven't been waiting for *that* long . . . !

The middle of the night where *you* are . . . ? Which is presumably in India . . . The Philippines? Why the Philippines . . . ?

Because wages have gone up in India – of course . . .

So if you'd just be kind enough to tell me what the emergency is that I'm calling about . . . Or what it *was* . . .

No, of course not – how could you know? My emergency, not yours! Fair enough!

So perhaps I could work it out if you simply told me what sort of emergency it is that this emergency helpline helps with . . . ?

With breakdowns? What – of cars . . . ? Oh – of people . . .

Of people who've been waiting to get through to emergency helplines . . .

Yes! Yes! Wait! Don't ring off . . . ! That *is* what I'm now calling about . . . !

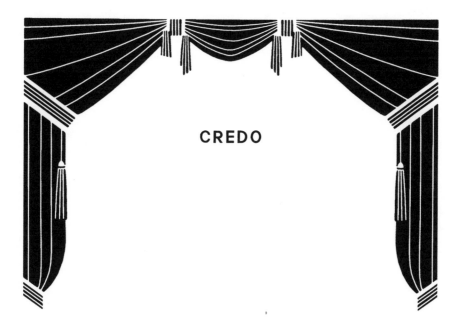

CREDO

I believe.

I believe in believing.

I believe in believers believing anything they want to believe, provided they believe *something*.

*

I believe in believers believing the believable, such as that spinach is good for you, and that white is white and black is black.

I also believe in believers half-believing the half-believable, such as theories to do with the Bermuda Triangle and the assassination of President Kennedy; or at any rate I half-believe it.

I also believe, though, that believing the believable is no great achievement, and half-believing the half-believable isn't much better, since even unbelievers believe the believable, and probably also half-believe a good few half-believable things as well.

I believe much more fervently in believers believing the totally unbelievable, such as that white is black and black is white; and that the world came into existence on February 17th, 1863; and that a medication made by waving a sprig of dogwort over a pint of tap water can cure baldness and prevent entropy.

I believe in believing that one of the benefits of believing the unbelievable is that it's good practice, so that once you have believed one unbelievable thing it strengthens your powers of belief to believe something even less believable, and perhaps one day win Olympic gold for believing.

*

I believe in believers believing that believers who believe the same beliefs as they themselves believe are true believers.

I believe in believers believing that believers who believe beliefs that they themselves do not believe are unbelievers.

I believe that believers who believe that other believers are unbelievers are fully justified in believing that these unbelievers should be beleaguered and belaboured by believers until the believers believe that the unbelievers believe.

I believe that believers should believe that even some of the believers they once believed had the same beliefs as themselves do in fact believe some slightly variant versions, and that they should therefore turn on them and beleaguer and belabour them as well.

I believe that the believers who are being beleaguered and belaboured by believers they once believed were their fellow-believers should beleaguer and belabour them back.

*

I believe that I have done quite enough believing for one day.

I believe that I should perhaps sit down now and have a cup of tea before I collapse with believer's burnout.

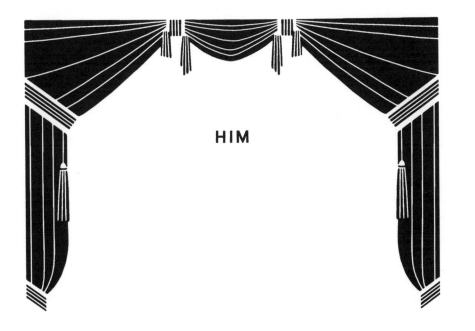

HIM

Excuse me! I don't want to be rude or anything, but my friend says it's you! We were just standing there and she suddenly screams, and I'm like, 'What? What is it?'

And she's like, 'Oh, my God! Oh, no! I don't believe it! It's him! It's him!'

And I'm like, 'Him? *Who's* him?'

And she's like, 'Over there! Him! Him! Him!'

And I look round and it's you and I'm like, 'What, *him*?'

And she's like, 'Him – yes! And it's him, it's him!'

And I'm like, 'Oh, my God, you don't mean . . . ?'

And she's like, 'Yes! Him!'

And I'm like, 'Oh, my God!'

And she's like, 'Or maybe it's *not* him . . .'

And I'm like, 'Ask him, ask him!'

And she's like, '*Ask* him?'

And I'm like, 'If it's him or not!'

And she's like, 'Oh, my God, I'll die! *You* ask him!'

And I'm like, '*I'm* not going to ask him!'

And she's like, 'Ask him! Ask him!'

And I'm like, 'No way!'

And she's like, 'No, go on – ask him!'

And I'm like, 'OK, I'll ask him.'

And she's like, 'No! No! Don't!'

And I'm like 'I am! I'm going to ask him!'

And she's like, 'Go on, then . . . ! No . . . ! Come back . . . ! No, all right . . .' Oh, you're not going . . . ? No, OK. No problem. Only . . . *were* you? *Were* you him . . . ?

OPEN SECRET

My firm has a security problem, and I'm hoping you're going to be able to help us. I know from your CV that you have a wide range of experience in these matters . . .

Our computers? No, no one's hacking into our computers. It's not a digital problem, it's a physical one . . . Our premises? No, our premises are well secured.

It's our products that are being broken into.

I assume that we're speaking in absolute confidence . . . ? Of course. Your trade, exactly. Your professional reputation. Thank you.

The point is this. We manufacture packaging. Little plastic bags to hold things like salted nuts or biscuits. The kind of thing you buy at the bar, or in a fast-food outlet. You must have bought them yourself many times . . . Anyway, those are our products. And you've found them, I hope, to be . . . ?

Completely impregnable. Thank you. I'm pleased to hear it. Kind of you to say so . . . Broken many a fingernail – wonderful . . . Loosened your front teeth . . . Good . . . Smashed one packet of biscuits against the bar in a fury . . . And crushed the entire contents to powder . . . This is so reassuring . . . ! Pulled the little red tabs we sometimes put on as decoys . . . And they've come away in your fingers . . . Tried stabbing them with your house keys . . . Left the keys on the bar – found yourself locked out . . .

The perfect customer!

But we're hearing worrying reports that some of our customers are not behaving quite so well. There are people out there who are actually managing to get packets open, in spite of all our efforts. Not usually men, who mostly stick with traditional techniques such as swearing and shouting and hurling the product across the room. Our packaging is still pretty resistant to this sort of approach. But there are women out there who are learning to use a cunning combination of patience and tools like nail-files and cuticle-trimmers.

Even more worrying: the police believe that there are criminal gangs from Eastern Europe operating in some places with electric drills and laser cutters. Shooting their way into slices of fruit cake, sometimes!

I don't have to tell you how important secure packaging is in protecting the public. Sweet biscuits cause obesity! Salty biscuits cause high blood pressure! If you've an allergy to nuts, breaking into a packet of cashews may be the last thing you do! You can choke to death on a potato crisp!

In any case it's not just a matter of the health or financial implications. We also have a very positive role to play in increasing the sum of human happiness. Because, good as I'm sure the food inside the packets is, if only you could get at it, there's no way in which it could ever be as good as you're hoping it will be. The longer we can defer the pleasure of actually eating it the more intense the anticipation. If we can postpone it forever, like the hope of heaven, we can raise the customers' pleasure to something like religious ecstasy.

You may not be aware that we also make mineral-water bottles. Spill mineral water on to a live electrical point and you can be electrocuted, which is why we make it impossible to unscrew the top without a monkey-wrench. Now we hear that people are taking monkey-wrenches with them when they go jogging!

Our packaging for things like freshly made pasta is still holding up fairly well. You know the things I mean? Plastic trays covered with a transparent plastic window that looks as though you should be able to peel it back, only you can't, you have to take a very sharp knife to it, and it slips, and goes into your hand, and you spend the evening sitting in A & E instead of eating ricotta-and-spinach agnolotti. So I don't think we need to make any changes here for the moment. Also our firm has just acquired a substantial interest in Lethal Kitchen Knives Ltd.

For which, incidentally, a substantial amount of business is also generated by our division making the shrink wrappings on DVDs. They look so flimsy, so easy to remove! But of course they're not! They're very difficult to find a way into! So once again you have to go out to the kitchen, and . . . Another five hours in A & E. 'You again! What is it this time? Prawn-and-pine-nut cappelletti . . . ? Oh – Highlights from *Aida* . . .'

So, what do we do? We can't very well put electronic alarms and guard dogs inside a packet of salted almonds! Anyway, you'll think about it and submit your proposals. And, listen: peanuts are just a beginning. Peanuts are peanuts! We're thinking big. Food and DVDs are not the only things that people are trying to open. There's also plays, bank accounts, dialogues, peace negotiations, Parliament. And mostly, when they succeed, with unforeseen and often downright disastrous results. If we could think of some form of unopenable packaging for all these other things as well we could make the world a safer and happier place.

Oh, and one final requirement – and this really in absolute confidence. Whatever you come up with to keep the general public out of the eatables, we have to continue giving the security services full access. GCHQ are very proud of storing the world's largest secret collection of dry-roasted Brazil nuts.

BACKDATE

Good morning, everyone, and welcome to our first production meeting!

So, OK, I'm directing the play, but contributions, please, from everyone! Let's kick it around a bit, folks, and let's be bold! Ideas, ideas, ideas! Nothing set in stone! Blue skies thinking! Outside the box! And the stalls and circle as well!

What's that, Literary Department . . . ? You haven't read it yet? Of course you haven't read it! *I* haven't read it. When did we start reading things? We're a theatre, not a ladies' reading group!

As the director I obviously want first and foremost to serve the play, blah blah blah. But I also want to make sure that the production gets noticed as a production. This team has a great record. No one's going to forget our *Gammer Gurton's Needle* set in Afghanistan, or our teenage *Lear*, or our *School for Scandal* in a school of dolphins.

So, a quick flick through the script as I stand here . . .

Do it all-men . . . ? Possibly. All-women . . . ? All-women but played by men, all-men but played by women . . . ? By women played by men cross-dressing as women . . . ?

It's set in the present, by the look of it . . . So that's our first problem. We can't update it to the present to make clear its relevance to our day and age if it's there already!

OK . . . Forget this day and age. We're going to make its relevance clear to some *other* day and age! Why should *this* day and age be privileged over any other? People in the past were also having a bad time! They also deserve to be made relevant to! So – the past, yes? As long as we shift it *somewhere*!

But, hey, there's an awful lot of the past! Which bit do we think most needs being made relevant to? Anyone?

What was that, Wardrobe? Still got all those SS uniforms left over from our *Puss in Boots* last Christmas? So you're saying Nazi? OK. *Puss* stirred them up a bit. Got the theatre picketed.

Or further back . . . 1920s? Hovis? We did *West Side Story* Hovis . . . Someone's saying beards and bustles . . . ? OK, as long as it's not doublet and hose! We might as well do suits and ties as doublet and hose.

So skip the sixteenth century . . . The thirteenth? What – the Black Death? Pustules, corpses? Make-up – are you cool with pustules . . . ?

Neolithic, why not . . . Paleolithic, even . . . Neanderthal . . . ? Could be sensational. No language. Just grunts, violence, sex . . .

Wait a moment, though. Universality. Are we achieving universality? Are we making this thing relevant not just to Neanderthals but to extraterrestrials . . . ? So – let's set it on another planet. In another galaxy . . . A parallel universe . . .

Sorry – someone at the back there trying to say something . . . Jane, isn't it? The girl doing work experience in Marketing . . . ? Hello, Jane . . . Yes, of course you may! Say whatever you want . . . Anything . . . Something outrageous? The more outrageous the better, Jane . . . !

Do it *how* . . . ? *As written* . . . ?

Jane, I know you've only been here for a week, and I don't want to discourage you, but that is quite frankly the most ridiculous suggestion I have ever heard.

Sure – I said 'outrageous'. But, Jane, 'as written . . .'! Let's not go *completely* insane! 'As written . . .' That is totally off the scale, Jane! It's frankly – yes – outrageous!

Outrageous, though . . . Wait a moment . . .

Jane, I love it!

SS uniforms back in the wardrobe! Parallel universe back in the scenery dock! As written, everyone, as written!

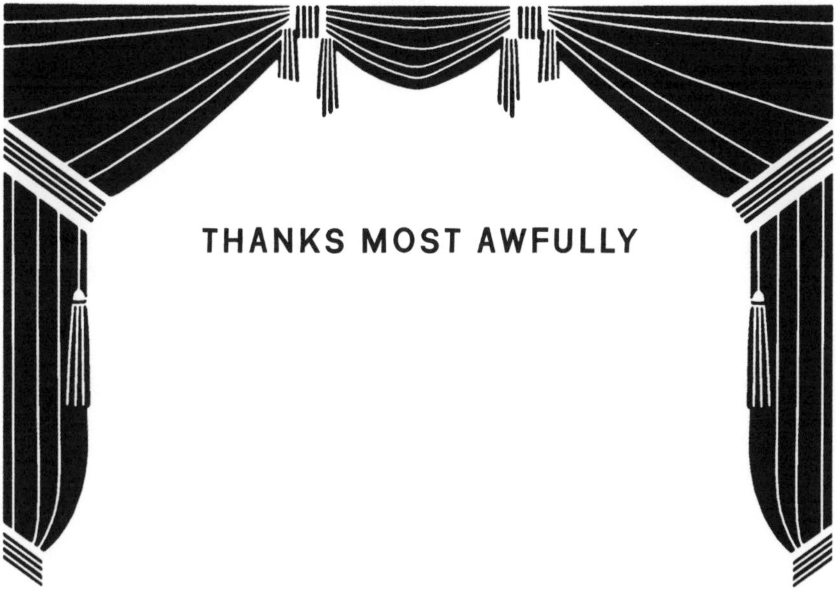
THANKS MOST AWFULLY

Thank You, Lord! For everything You've done for me in life!

First of all, of course, for my daily bread. Not to mention the butter and organic honey to put on it! Also, of course, for my five portions of green vegetables and fruit per day, without which I should probably not be as fit and as able to express my gratitude to You as I am!

While I'm in the food and drink section of my prayers I should perhaps also mention coffee (Fairtrade, of course!) which in moderate amounts I believe is now thought to reduce the risk of Alzheimer's. Oh, and my occasional glass of some modest but reasonably drinkable claret, which, provided I don't drink so much of it that it damages my liver, helps to preserve some other organ, though I can't remember now whether it's my heart or my brain (which may suggest, if the latter, that I'm not drinking quite enough of it!).

Thank You also, of course, Lord, for clothes to my back and a roof over my head. And, it seems only common sense to add, for laundry and dry cleaning to maintain the clothes, and insulating materials to make the roof more ecologically acceptable.

You have, of course, bestowed similar benefits upon many millions of other people as well – though not, very understandably, given the numbers involved, upon everyone. But I want to take the chance today to say thank You also for the more individual gifts You have singled me out to receive. It's not of course for me to judge whether I have a talent for seeing the best in everything, as people tell me, together with a kind heart and a wonderful sense of humour, but if You agree with their assessment it would be presumptuous of me to disagree, and plainly I owe it all to You.

As I do my ability actually to express the gratitude I feel, which I know some people find difficult. (When I think of all I have done to help my brother with his various problems, for example, and how I have never had so much as a word of thanks from him . . . However, forbearance is certainly another of my traits – and one for which I'm also deeply grateful.)

Quite *why* You've been so munificent to me I really don't know! As we have been told so many times, though, You move in mysterious ways, and trying to guess what You're up to in this particular case would be impertinent. You must have Your reasons! So let me just say a great big heartfelt thank-You and leave it at that!

I have, needless to say, also many shortcomings – and I'd like to say a special word of thanks to You for being so understanding about them. For not being too literal-minded, in the first place, about my failure to give all that I have to the poor. You haven't said anything specific about this – or indeed about anything else! – but I get the impression from Your silence that You do realise how substantial are the contributions I make to Oxfam and the local church restoration fund, among many other good causes. I always, of course, conscientiously complete the various Gift Aid certificates, and I have the feeling that You're prepared to accept that this can count towards the proportion of my income that I give to charity.

It's still a long way short of 100 per cent, which the New Testament suggests as an appropriate level, but, as You know, things have changed a bit since those days. 'Give all thou hast to the poor' – fine, but I think 'all thou hast' in this context probably meant a few coins tucked away in an earthenware pot, not the kind of money that people have in their bank accounts and share portfolios these days. If the Lord had foreseen the dramatic increase in so many people's personal wealth over the next two thousand years he might have been prepared to accept a considerably lower percentage. Even 2 or 3 per cent, say, of an income perhaps measured in millions and tens of millions of pounds, he might have felt, would have been more than adequate to meet his general point.

I assume he was in any case thinking of *net* wealth, after due allowance had been made for tax, health scheme contributions, school and university fees, etc. Maintenance and cleaning. Gas, electric, and grocery bills. Depreciation on car, etc.

He would certainly have understood that if everyone started to raise cash for the poor by selling their entire holding of stocks and shares the market would collapse, and pretty soon, even if people paid out the whole 100 per cent, it would be 100 per cent of nothing at all.

I think I also detect a pragmatic approach on Your part not just to money, but to many other questions besides. The Ten Commandments, for example. In my case, since I do pretty well on honouring my father and mother, I think I have Your tacit agreement that I'm allowed a little leeway in other directions.

I don't mean it's all right for me to go around murdering people, but I think I can probably do a little bit of coveting, can't I, without completely unbalancing the moral budget? My next-door neighbour's new sun lounge, for instance. And that rather disturbingly attractive new wife of his, provided she doesn't realise I can see into the sun lounge out of the spare-bedroom window . . .

I suspect that You take much the same attitude as the tax people. Provided You get a reasonable proportion of what You're owed You'll probably compound for the rest rather than prosecute, which might kill off a valuable source of moral income.

All things are from God! So a final word of thanks for letting me fall off that ladder last week and break my ankle. Very painful! But it gave me a welcome chance to demonstrate once again, as I hobble around on my crutches, my remarkable cheerfulness and submission to Your will. And thereby to improve even further upon the very satisfactory moral character You gave me.

Also yes – to exercise once again my remarkable capacity for being grateful!

SPONSOR ME!

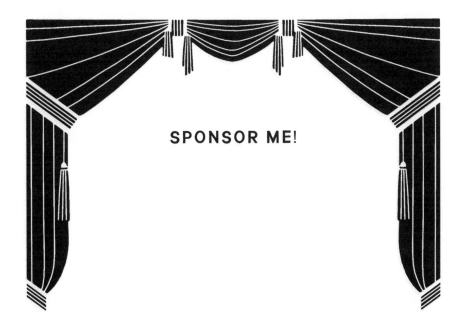

Will you?

I don't mean to run the marathon. Or to swim from here to there, or to cycle from there to here. Or to climb Everest, or to jump out of an aircraft with a dodgy parachute and only half an hour's training.

I mean, will you sponsor me *not* to run the marathon? *Not* to cycle anywhere or to climb anything or to do anything else I don't actually want to do?

To just sit quietly in an armchair, and perhaps read a book or watch something on television. To do a bit of work and earn myself a living, then sleep as soundly as I can at night. To eat breakfast, lunch, tea, and dinner. Perhaps, if you'd be kind enough to make it worth my while, to drink an occasional glass of wine.

In other words, to do what I was going to be doing anyway. And to restrain myself from doing anything that involves road closures. Or crashing up and down the local swimming pool and colliding with nervous and vulnerable young people learning to swim, which would perhaps put them off for life.

Or falling off my bicycle and adding to the burden of some overworked A & E department, then occupying a hospital bed that could have been occupied by someone else who *had* been sponsored to climb Everest, and had as a result got frostbite or heart failure, then been repatriated in a specially chartered private plane, which could therefore not be used for flying bankers or industrialists to meetings with other bankers or industrialists, and enabling all of them to make even more money than before, and to pay even less tax, and as a result to be in a position to sponsor even more people to do even more ridiculous things and cause even more trouble.

Will you sponsor me not to risk shortening my life in one way or another, and thereby making myself unavailable to support the nation's economic recovery? And at the same time, of course, reducing the time available to support it still further by going out to the shops and buying things?

You *would* be prepared to? Of course you would! You'd be delighted to find such a socially valuable way to indulge your charitable instincts!

And this is for a really good cause! The money will go towards sponsoring other people not to let themselves be sponsored to do things that close roads, fill hospitals, etc.

Dare I trespass on your generosity even further, and ask if you would sponsor me for a little more if I undertook to do even *less* than usual? Not to go out of the house at all? Not to get out of bed?

Wonderful! That's so kind of you! And you might even feel inspired to ask me to sponsor *you*. To do what? The same, of course – nothing!

And naturally I should be delighted. If you would be prepared to sponsor me to sponsor you.

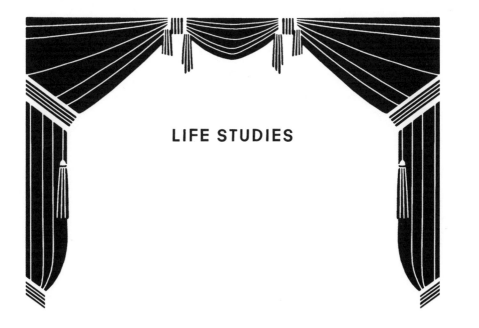

LIFE STUDIES

Henry, yes, Henry Sneed, but just Henry, of course! And you're Jane Tubbs? Nice to meet you, Jane! You find such interesting people through Great Dates! My last date was a woman who recycled plastic clothes-hangers, and the one before supplied replacement parts for yoghurt machines! And the introduction says that you teach creative writing!

> – Well, I simply try to help people get their ideas into publishable shape.

Wow! What – life studies, that sort of thing?

> – Mostly, yes. So tell me about *your* life.

My life? Oh, well, all rather ordinary, I'm afraid. I'm a piano salesman.

> – Fascinating! And of course you play?

Play what?

– The piano!

Oh. Not really. Well, just a bit. To demonstrate to customers.

– But, before your breakdown . . . ?

My breakdown? What breakdown? Oh, you mean the car? When I had to get Home Start?

– In the middle of your performance, Spencer! At Carnegie Hall! Carnegie Hall would be good. We have to think about your American readers, Spencer!

Well, Henry, actually.

– I think Spencer. They won't believe Henry. No one's called Henry. So after the breakdown – what? A clinic in Switzerland? We have to keep in mind the locations, Spencer, for when they make the film.

Yes, but hold on . . .

– And out it all comes. How you were abused by your parents.

Abused by my parents?

– They never went on at you about tidying your room?

Well, yes, but . . .

– Spencer, you still have the mental scars! Your lifelong battle with alcoholism for a start! Don't tell me it's just a glass of ginger wine at Christmas, Spencer. It's two glasses, it's three glasses! It's a shandy on your summer holidays! And the drug abuse, Spencer! That time you had a headache, remember, and you went to the bathroom cabinet to take two soluble aspirins. Only you miscounted and took three! And when was this? It was in the eighties, wasn't it? Madonna! Whitney Houston! Those wild nights watching them on television! Have you ever publicly acknowledged paternity?

Paternity?

– Of your love-child, Spencer!

My . . . what?

Oh, so you're still denying it, are you? Spencer, you're living a lie!
This is why you took to haunting sordid clubs and bars! Don't deny
it, Spencer, because you're in one now!

Starbucks?

– And what are you doing in Starbucks, Spencer? You're letting
yourself get picked up by the notorious Domina Trix!

I thought your name was Jane something . . .

– A teacher of creative writing and I can't create a name for myself?
You're strangely drawn to me. You feel as if your whole life is being
taken over. You leave your wife . . .

I'm not married!

[92]

– That's what they all say!

No, but that's why I've subscribed to Great Dates!

– And that's why we understand each other – because we're both liars and fantasists! So when I come up with this plot to murder your wife . . .

No wife! Not married!

– Oh, you've murdered her already, have you? That's good, Spencer. A bit of plot under your belt before we start. And now of course you need me to help you vanish. I invent a new identity for you. You become . . . you become . . . yes . . . Henry Sneed! A piano salesman with a happy childhood, who drinks ginger wine at Christmas! The kind of man who arranges to meet supposed creative writing teachers in Starbucks! Then – listen to this, you're not going to believe this! – one day you find her – you find me, your creative writing teacher – in bed with your wife! She and I have set up the whole murder story together simply to get you out of the way and take over your bank account! How about that?

But . . .

– You love it! Now, get this! It's a double bluff! I'm only sleeping with your wife to get my hands on her share of the money she's stolen off you! Is that good? Are we creating something like a credible human life story here?

Well, possibly. But I thought you said I'd murdered my wife?

– Did I? Oh, yes, you murdered her . . . No! Listen, Spencer – listen, Henry. You *thought* you'd murdered her, but you hadn't, because I'd switched the poison! It wasn't a double bluff – it was a triple! In fact you gave her a harmless mango smoothie!

No, I didn't!

> – I beg your pardon? Who's in charge of this life of yours? You or
> me? I'm telling you you did!

No, because what I did in fact was, I pushed her down the cellar steps!

> – You . . . what?

I pushed her down the cellar steps!

> – You – pushed your wife down the cellar steps? What are you
> saying, Henry? That you killed your wife?

No, no, no! She slipped, she slipped! Anyway, she was never near the
cellar steps! We have no cellar steps! And she's perfectly well! She's
living in Argentina! I had a postcard from her only last week! And it was
the au pair who pushed her! And I never had a wife in the first place!

> – Hold on, hold on. I'm losing the plot here . . .

But never mind about *my* life. You haven't told me anything about yours. Let me guess . . . Born in Thornton Heath. Brownies and Girl Guides. Engaged for seven years to the manager of the local Co-op. Part-time creative writing teacher, part-time chiropodist. Until one day it all changes. You meet this psychopathic liar and wife-murderer in Starbucks, and you become a completely different person. He helps you write your memoirs. He takes 50 per cent of first serial, film, television, and merchandising rights, and lives happily ever after . . . And what do you do? You refund his expenses. Two soya milk lattes. Five pounds twenty. In cash, please.

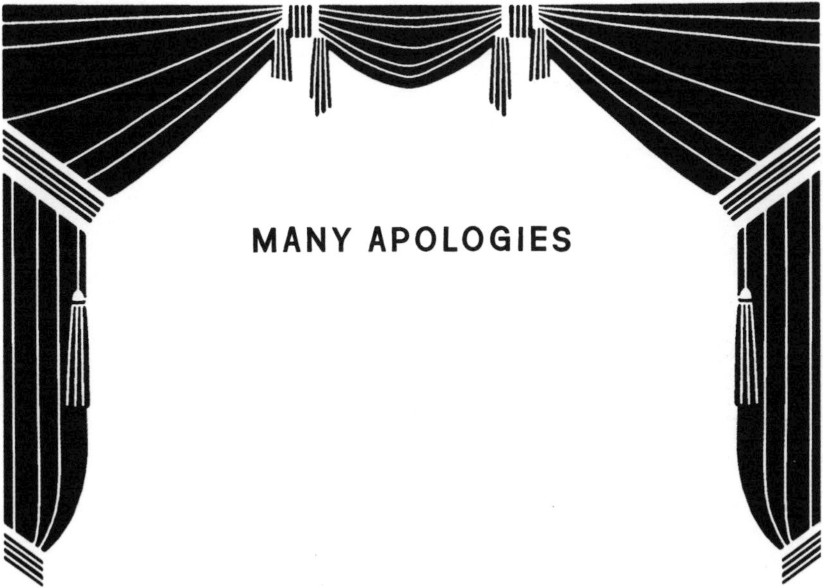

MANY APOLOGIES

We apologise for any inconvenience caused.

You've seen that said so many times that you probably didn't even notice it sitting there on the page, so we'll say it again:

We apologise for any inconvenience caused.

In fact you've seen it so many times that you probably think it doesn't mean anything. You don't believe we're really apologising at all. You don't believe we actually care tuppence about all this inconvenience we're causing.

Well, that may be the case when some firms say it. Eeziphit Phootware and Sprew Brothers spring to mind! But we can assure you that at Straygate and Hapstraw we're not like that. We really do feel bad about the way we're behaving!

But, even so, when we say 'We apologise,' you don't believe that we actually mean 'we'. Not *all* of us, surely! Not everyone in the firm!

We mean just that. *Everyone* at Straygate and Hapstraw. Everyone at Head Office, everyone in all seven branch offices, everyone in the works and the transport division.

Take Mr Hoggin, for instance, Sales Director (West Midlands). He hasn't slept for the last three nights, he's so upset. Or the Director of Human Resources – he's had to get professional counselling. The Chairman himself has been seen crying in the corridor – and he's never cried before, not even when we dropped a whole lorry-load of semi-processed animal waste on the M1, and caused a tailback from Watford Gap to Leicester Forest.

That's as may be, you say. But even if everyone feels it, it can't be everyone who's actually *saying* it. The only person actually saying these words is just that new intern in the public relations department. They've left her in the office on her own to say all this while the rest of them go off to suffer their various guilt feelings in private.

Well, since we're being absolutely frank and honest here . . . You're right – it *is* the new intern. Me – Kate. Hi! It's me actually uttering the words, yes – but only because we can't all utter them at the same time together! We've got thirty-seven people working at Head Office alone! You can't have thirty-seven people chanting 'We apologise for any inconvenience caused' in unison! You can't have 370 fingers on the same keyboard! I can assure you, though, that everyone is crowding round the desk, apologising in their own time and their own way, and begging to be associated with everything we're saying. OK – with everything *I'm* saying.

Well, they *were* crowding round my desk, but it's six o'clock now and they've all gone off to the pub to drown their sorrows. And left Muggins here holding the baby. Once again.

Not that our apology would be any more sincere or grovelling if we'd all stayed in after work to make it. In fact we might start to feel resentful instead of apologetic.

I wish I could be more specific about what exactly the inconvenience is that we're apologising for. They were all too upset to explain properly. It's something really bad this time, I know. Unless they were just winding me up . . . Something worse than last time, probably, when we burst a water main and submerged the whole of Leamington Spa . . . No, that was the time before last. The last time was – oh, my God, how could I forget? – when we somehow started a war somewhere, I think in East Africa.

Whatever it is this time, we didn't mean to do it, I can tell you that.

We make such efforts not to be a nuisance! And most of the time we succeed. We're good as gold. But sometimes we just *have* to cause a bit of inconvenience if we're going to get anything done in the world! Or we simply make a mistake, and press the wrong button. Or some demon gets into us, you know how it is.

If only I knew exactly what we'd done I could make some attempt to explain the psychology behind it. But you probably wouldn't believe it. And it would just take up even more of your time. We feel bad enough about your having to listen to all this, believe us.

None of this, of course, is to be taken as admitting liability! Let's get that quite straight! Feeling bad about something doesn't mean we want to pay out hundreds of thousands of pounds in damages!

That would just make us feel even worse.

GOING FOR GOLD

Good evening, and welcome to the National Semi-Finals of the UK TV-watching Championships!

Behind me you can see our four semi-finalists, all looking a little tense as we wait for slumpdown. Dawn Dreem there warming up with a few yawns – the judges are going to be giving extra points this year for yawning . . . Bob Scrum just relaxedly opening and closing his eyes . . . Rona Threw in a close huddle with her trainer and back-up team . . . Even the unflappable Norris Ogg being given a bit of last-minute massage on his bottom in preparation for the gruelling five days ahead.

While we're waiting we're joined by last year's winner, veteran TV-watcher Miles Tooley. Miles, I believe you started watching TV in the days when people used to do it for fun? Difficult for some of the youngsters to believe now! People would simply sit there in front of the screen, and just – what – *enjoy* it?

– I don't know about *enjoy* it, Ed. Things weren't quite that bad! But it certainly felt a bit self-indulgent. You were watching all these people on the screen in front of you straining every muscle to be best at dancing, or ice-skating, or surviving in the jungle – and there you were yourself, sitting on the sofa with a bag of nuts, watching them.

So, no league tables? No effort to please the fans?

– No fans! No one watching anyone watch! You were just out there on your own, doing it!

Difficult to achieve excellence, I imagine, with no one to compare yourself to?

– Excellence? We didn't know what excellence in TV-watching was! Of course you have to remember that this was only a few years after people gave up dancing because they liked dancing.

And cooking, so someone told me, because they liked cooking!

– Yes. Or eating the result! And we didn't even have competitive eating in those days! People would eat just because they liked eating. Or for some other entirely selfish reason, like wanting to stay alive.

I know you've sometimes worried about all the ordinary Joes out there who feel they're not up to eating at competition standard.

– We have to be inclusive, Ed, and eating's a pretty tough sport when you take it seriously! I've seen people choke to death in the speed-eating events. Which is why I was so pleased when the first sneezing championships started up.

And then, of course, passing wind . . .

– Bullying, washing up, falling down drunk in the street . . .

Miles, I'm going to interrupt you there, because I think we have . . . Yes! Slumpdown! And a great start there by Bob Scrum, slipping down very attractively until his back's almost completely horizontal . . .

– He made his reputation on armchair, of course, but this season he's been playing almost equally well on sofa.

Nice sequence of co-ordinated yawns there from Dawn Dreem . . . Oh, and a beautifully judged snide comment from Norris Ogg!

– Norris, of course, was runner-up in snide comments in the Southern Hemisphere Championships in Melbourne last year, but he had a bad patch at the Birmingham games, when one of the judges alleged he'd heard him make a couple of approving remarks.

Interesting to note that those are the same viewing socks he was wearing when he won at Buenos Aires last year. And now – yes – Rona Threw's mouth is beginning to fall open! The excitement building here as it edges ever wider!

– You can see on the action replay what a beautifully graduated movement it is . . .

I should say about, what, 2.15 centimetres? The judges are measuring it now.

– She achieved 2.21 centimetres in Melbourne, of course.

The figures are just going up . . . And it's 2.17 centimetres! Only five minutes into the first round, and Rona Threw has already put up this jaw-cracking figure!

– But can she maintain the gruelling pace for another five days?

And while we're waiting to find out we're joined by Hans van Flogg, the chairman of the World TV-watching Organisation. Hans, I know the organisation has been involved in a number of controversial decisions recently, such as disqualifying the entire French national team for using illegal soporifics, but leave that aside for the moment. What of the future? What can the organisation do to involve all those ordinary fans who can't manage to watch TV to competition standards?

– What we're working towards, Ed, is competitively doing
absolutely nothing at all, not even watching the TV-watching.

Who can breathe the least without actually quite dropping dead?

– Exactly. And then – who knows? – actually dropping dead, with
gold beckoning for dropping deadest!

I KNOW I KNOW

Darling, you remember that man we met?

   – What man?

At that thing we went to.

   – You mean that thing at the wherever it was?

Yes, and we met that man. You know who I mean?

   – Yes, yes.

You do remember him?

   – What, that man we met? Of course I remember him! Why do you
   think I might not remember him? You're always treating me as if
   I'm senile!

Yes, well, as long as you do remember him . . .

   – Perfectly. So what about him?

What was his name?

– His *name*?

His name, yes.

– You want to know his name?

Yes, but since you obviously don't know . . .

– I *do* know!

Go on, then.

– I don't know it just at this precise moment. I *did* know.

You've stopped knowing?

– Yes, because you just suddenly . . .

. . . *asked* you.

– You're always doing this! Just suddenly asking me things!

So if I hadn't just suddenly asked you . . . ?

– I could have told you. Of course!

But if I hadn't asked you you wouldn't have known I wanted to know!

– No, so then it wouldn't have driven it out of my head.

Anyway, you *don't* know.

– I *do* know! I know it as well as I know my own name!

Which is what, incidentally?

– Don't! Please! Even as a joke. Because I *will*! I'll forget my own name, if you just suddenly *ask* me!

I see. I mustn't just suddenly ask you things. So how do you want me to ask you?

– Well . . . gradually. In a roundabout way. Not in the form of a *question*. Talk about something else.

Something else?

– All the various people we've met in the last few weeks. And then say something like, 'For instance, there was that man we met at that thing.' And I say, 'What, you mean Tim?'

Tim?

– *Tim!* Yes! There you are, you see! Tim Thompson! I *knew* I knew!

Oh, of course. Thank you. Robin Roughly.

– Robin Roughly?

As soon as you said Tim Thompson I remembered at once.

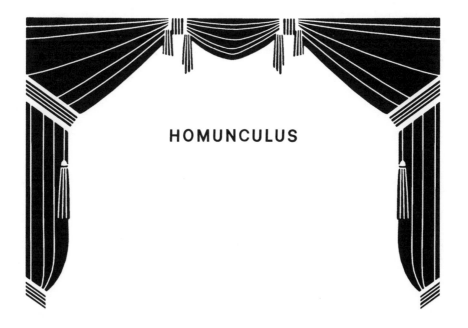

HOMUNCULUS

Hello . . . ? Speaking . . .

The manager? Am I the manager? Me? What would I be manager of . . . ?
Of the *theatre*? Of *what* theatre . . . ?

The Cartesian Theatre? Oh, I see. You mean the theatre inside my head?
The one with a little man sitting inside it watching all the input from my
five senses and telling me what to do about it? The thing that explains
why I'm conscious and the computer in front of me isn't . . . ?

Yes, well, let me tell you something: it doesn't exist! It's a satirical fiction!
It's just a device to debunk the mind/body dualism that seems to linger
in the writings of various neurologists and . . . Oh, you've read about it
. . . Exactly! So you know that there *is* no Cartesian Theatre! There *is* no
little man . . . !

Who *are* you, anyway . . . ? You're what . . . ? You're the little man?

Oh.

So where are you calling from . . . ? The payphone in the foyer . . . In what foyer . . . ? Of the Cartesian Theatre . . . ? Not the one in *my* head, I hope . . . ! Oh, it *is* the one in *my* head.

Which doesn't exist . . . ! And which is also what . . . ? In a very rundown condition . . . ? Broken seats . . . Crumbling gilt mouldings . . . Filthy toilets . . .

Is this a complaint . . . ? A warning. I see. You're going to get the inspectors on to me . . .

What – telling you that you don't exist? That made you even angrier, did it? Well, I'm sorry, but . . . Also you don't like being called a homunculus. Who called you a homunculus . . . ? Oh, some philosopher did. Not me, though, obviously! Since you don't exist. You should be grateful! If *I* didn't exist and someone called me a homunculus, I'd take that as something of a concession . . .

Any other complaints, while we're about it? The quality of the entertainment, perhaps? Nothing worth watching these days? All repeats . . . ?

I thought so . . . *Why* did I think so? Because you just sound like the sort of person who goes round saying that there's nothing worth watching these days . . . Oh, and you find some of the conversations I have with my friends pretty boring, do you? Also better in the old days, presumably. When it was all in black and white . . .

You liked some of those experiences I had when I was young, and I used to meet different girls and so on . . . Yes, thank you, never mind the details. But how about the comedy? You like that, don't you . . . ? What about the night when I went to put the milk bottles out and the front door shut behind me? And it was mid-winter and I was in my pyjamas and I had to go to next door's and the woman thought . . .

OK, yes, a bit formulaic. Seen it before. I accept that. But you laughed! You did! I know you did, because I heard you . . . !

Yes, even though you don't exist.

But your wife likes the wildlife ones, at any rate. The squirrels digging up the daffodils and so on . . . So at least you've got your wife with you in there . . . *And* your children . . . ? Four of them . . . ? Three girls and a boy! Wonderful . . . Not just a little man! A whole little family in there . . . !

What – 'little'? You *said*! 'I'm the little man . . .'! Oh, all right for *you* to say it. But if *I* say it . . . Sizeism. Yes, of course. I'm sorry . . . No, I understand . . . And Katie's already as tall as her mother . . .

Shocked, are they? By some of the language . . . ? I'm sorry, but it's what I hear! It's what people are saying out there! That's the world we live in! You wouldn't want me to make it all up, would you . . . ? Some things I make up, yes, of course . . . And you also have to watch all that, do you . . . ? A lot of it pretty unsuitable for younger viewers . . . ?

I get the point – you don't like the job. Not too bad, I should have thought, as jobs go. Nice warm theatre to sit in. And you get a break from time to time . . . Well, at night, for instance . . . Yes, I suppose there's dreams . . . And insomnia . . . Not much fun, no, watching the sort of stuff that's going through my head at four in the morning.

Look, if the work's really so awful go and find another job! Because it's ridiculous! You don't exist and I wouldn't need you even if you did! There are plenty of other ways of accounting for consciousness!

What other ways . . . ? Well . . .

Yes, that theory's one of the leading contenders, certainly . . . All right, if you don't like that one there's also . . . Exactly! And then how about . . . ? That one, yes . . . Don't make you what . . . ? Laugh?

Well, I find *your* claims pretty hilarious, I have to tell you. Because if I needed to employ you to explain how I was conscious you'd need to have a little man inside you in your turn to explain how *you* were conscious, and another little man inside him, and . . . Exactly . . . !

You *have* got a little man inside you . . . ? And the theatre inside *his* head has been completely reupholstered and regilded, and there's proper Dyson Airblade hand driers in the toilets, plus he gets four weeks paid holiday per annum . . . ?

So go ahead and get a job inside your own head, if the conditions are so marvellous . . . ! Yes, right now! Get out! Beat it! You're fired!

Hello . . . ? Hello . . . ? What's happened? We've got cut off. I can't hear anything . . .

I can't *see* anything! I've gone blind! I can't feel anything! I can't think anything . . . !

Listen – come back! I apologise! I'm sorry . . . !

Oh my God, no – I'm not even sorry . . . !

ARE YOU SITTING
COMFORTABLY?

I'm going to tell you a story.

   – You're going to *what*?

Tell you a story.

   – What's all this about?

Nothing. I just thought you might enjoy it.

   – A *story*?

A story, yes! All right?

   – Hold on. What sort of story? You mean a joke? This feller walks
   into a bar, says to the barman? There's this little Jewish guy and he
   says to this Irish feller?

Not a joke, no.

– So, what, you mean a true story? You were just walking along the street the other day minding your own business when suddenly?

No, no – a made-up story.

– A *made-up* story? Made up by who?

By me! All right? All right . . .

– Wait, wait. You know how to make up stories, do you?

No! I've never done it before!

– Oh. You mean, you just suddenly . . . ?

Yes! Just suddenly thought I would! So . . .

– Hold on, hold on. You're not selling something? It's not some kind of scam?

No! I'm just . . . *doing* it! For fun! For no reason! So, here we go . . .

– It's not a ghost story? Something spooky happened in the middle of the night, and when you woke up in the morning you were dead?

I don't think it's going to be a ghost story, no.

– You don't *think* it is! You mean you don't know?

Not yet, no.

– You're just going to . . . start saying something . . . ?

And see what happens! Yes!

– All right. As long as it's not a ghost story. Or about dogs or rabbits. Or anything heartwarming.

Just wait and you'll find out. We'll *both* find out!

– May I make a suggestion, though? Could it be about this man, and he's a scientist, and he has this plan to be master of the universe,

and he's called something like Z, and he builds this kind of secret
ray thing, only there's this woman called something like Purpurilla,
and she wears this kind of shiny silver leotard thing and these high-
heeled boots, and she can dematerialise and rematerialise, and go
backwards and forwards in time . . .

Right. Thank you. I'll keep it in mind.

– . . . and they're in this kind of enormous glass casino thing,
drinking champagne, and there are these giant spiders which have
had kind of chips inserted in their brains . . .

Good. Wonderful. Now *my* story begins in a little whitewashed cottage in
a forest . . .

– . . . and this Z person escapes into a kind of secret tunnel in the
fabric of space-time . . .

Yes, and in this cottage lives a little old woman who has a tabby cat . . .

– . . . and, wait, because this is getting interesting! I'm beginning to enjoy myself!

Yes, but I'm not. I don't actually like listening to stories.

– No, nor do I!

Never mind. Just this once. You can tell me yours tomorrow. So one day the little old woman says to the cat, 'Now, pussy dear, I have to go and milk the cow to get you some cream for your tea . . .'

– So there they are, in this alternative universe thing . . .

I'm not listening!

– And there's this weird man who tries to tell someone a story . . .

I've got my hands over my ears!

– . . . only this person he's telling the story to starts telling a story himself, and he suddenly realises it's what he's always wanted to do in life, and it completely transforms his character, and he starts writing bestsellers and he becomes very rich and famous, and . . . hello . . . ? Are you there . . . ? You haven't gone, have you . . . ? I'm not talking to myself . . . ?

MY MEETING WITH MOZART

Mozart? You're *Mozart* . . . ?

Always so much noise at parties like this . . . I thought for a moment you said you were *Mozart* . . . !

You *did* say you were Mozart . . . ? Oh. Presumably not *the* Mozart! Not Wolfgang Amadeus . . . ?

You *are*! You're Wolfgang Amadeus Mozart? But not the one who wrote . . . oh, what's it called . . . ? What do I mean? I'm so thrown – everything's gone out of my head . . .

Eine kleine Nachtmusik? Well, yes, for instance. You're not the Mozart who wrote *Eine kleine Nachtmusik*!

You are? You wrote *Eine kleine Nachtmusik* . . . ?

You wish what . . . ? That I wouldn't keep saying *Eine kleine Nachtmusik* . . . ? You're a bit fed up with people coming up to you and they can't remember anything you've written except *Eine kleine Nachtmusik*? I can imagine!

Anyway, though, you're Mozart . . . Of course I believe you . . . ! Don't you *look* like Mozart? Oh, sure, you *look* like Mozart. Perruque, knee breeches, and so on. But surely you're – I don't know quite how to put this – but aren't you, you know . . . ?

Dead? Well – yes! Dead!

No – I can see *you're* not dead . . . ! That's my point . . . ! Not even slightly dead! Very much alive! Old? No – not old at all! Just a bit – you know –

perruque and knee breeches! But in yourself, no – positively youthful!

Let me just get this absolutely straight. You're saying that you're the Mozart who wrote . . . ? Yes, yes – but also all the operas, all the symphonies . . . ?

Symphony No. 1, first of all? Exactly . . . Then Symphony No. 2 – of course. And so on, and so on . . .

No. 18 – yes . . . No. 19 . . . Yes, yes – I've got the point . . . No. 36, No. 37, exactly . . .

My God, it's just getting to me! I'm standing here talking to Mozart!

And now of course I don't know what to say! I mean, the greatest . . . the most wonderful . . . I mean – *Mozart*! And here I am *talking* to you!

I've got all your records . . . ! The operas – the chamber music – the piano concertos . . . !

So don't I like the what . . . ? The sacred music? Of course I like the sacred music . . . ! Why do you think I don't like the sacred music . . . ? I didn't mention it – no – I just hadn't got to it! I think the C major Mass is possibly the very greatest thing you ever . . . I mean, not greater than everything else! It's all great!

So many things I've always wanted to say to you, and suddenly here you are, and I'm tongue-tied – I can't think of any of them!

I'm such a fan! No, not just a *fan* – that's ridiculous – I'm an absolute . . . I don't know how to put this . . . I mean, the late piano concertos, for a start! No. 24, in D minor – no, D major . . . What . . . ? C minor? C minor – yes – I mean C minor . . . And that bit in *Don Giovanni* where she comes in, what's she called, I can't remember her name, I've forgotten all their names, but she goes . . . No, no – she goes . . . I can hear it in my head, I just can't . . . Sorry. You must absolutely hate this, going to parties and you meet this person who tries to sing your own things to you . . .

Never mind *Giovanni*. What about that bit in *Fidelio* . . . ! Sublime! Perhaps that really is the very greatest moment out of everything that you . . .

Beethoven? That was Beethoven . . . ? *Fidelio*? Did I say *Fidelio*? I didn't say *Fidelio*! Did I? Of course I know it was Beethoven who wrote *Fidelio*! I didn't mean *Fidelio*! *Figaro* is what I was trying to say! *Figaro, Figaro, Figaro* . . . ! *Figaro qui, Figaro là* . . . ! No, no – not you, I know, *that* particular number . . . Rossini, yes – *The Barber of Seville* – I know, I know! I meant, I didn't mean . . . I meant . . .

Anyway, Beethoven, since we mentioned Beethoven. What do you think of Beethoven? And Wagner? Schoenberg? Boulez? I can't believe I'm standing here listening to you telling me what you think of Boulez! Except you're not, because I'm babbling away so wildly you can't get a word in edgeways! I'm going to wake up in the middle of the night and remember this conversation and I'm going to shoot myself!

Can I at least have your autograph . . . ? Oh, wonderful . . . If I can just find something to write on . . . One of your CDs, obviously, but . . . Not *on* me, no, quite . . . Here we are – in my ticket pocket – old ticket stub . . . *Fidelio.* Of course – it just would have to be *Fidelio* . . .

Oh my God, don't look . . . ! Too late – she's spotted us! Some woman I used to know! She's coming over! I'm going to have to introduce you, and I can't remember her name . . . !

No – got it! Wendela . . . Wendela something . . .

Wendela, darling! How lovely to see you . . . ! This is my old friend
Wendela . . . Wendela . . . Wendela *Wheedle* . . . Wendela, you're not
going to believe this, but may I introduce – fanfare of authentic baroque
trumpets! – may I introduce . . . ?

May I introduce . . . ?

I'm terribly sorry – this can't be happening to me! – I'm going to have to
ask you to tell me your name again . . .

STILL LIFE

Hi. Where's Mrs Thatcher today, then?

> – Maggie? She's gone down the job centre. Bastards have stopped her jobseeker's.

So this pitch is free?

> – All yours. Whoever you are.

That's one of the things I hate about this line of work, not being able to turn your head, see who's working next to you.

> – I know your voice, though. Charlie Chaplin, aren't you?

Was. Last year. No one's Charlie Chaplin now.

> – So now you're . . . ?

No one.

> – No one? Oh.

Bloke.

    – Broke?

Bloke.

    – That's what *I* hate about the work – trying to speak without
moving your lips. So, you're a bloke? You mean just an ordinary
bloke? What, leaning on a shovel? Up in the air? No visible means
of support?

That's what the punters are looking for now.

    – Good up there, is it?

Get more of a view. And it's a bit further away from the punters. You
want to try it some time.

    – Not me. No head for heights.

So you're still – sorry, can't turn *my* head now I'm up here – Batman, isn't it?

    – Superman.

Superman. Lovely. Takes me back . . . Hold on, though. I can hear one or two punters coming . . .

*

Sounded like a quid.

    – In *your* tin. Sounded like 2p in mine.

What, you bent down? Shook their hand? And got 2p?

    – *You* bent down, did you?

Can't bend down, if you're hanging in space.

– You did something. I heard you.

Oh – turned upside down.

– Turned upside down? That's what the bastards want these days, is it? Aerobatics? I'd need a sick bag.

Sh. A few more of them coming . . .

*

What – nothing? You looped the loop for them up there, and they walked right past?

– They didn't even look at me.

They're frightened that if they look at you they'll have to give you something.

– And they're frightened it might put us off.

Make us self-conscious.

– We'd move, and it would be their fault.

They can't bear the strain.

– There we are, up on the stand, up in the sky, struggling not to blink.

Not to sneeze.

– Not to twitch.

And there *they* are, walking round blinking away to their heart's content.

– Sneezing their heads off.

Twitching . . .

– Scratching . . .

So they feel guilty . . .

– Which is the only reason they ever cough up.

No one realises how much people move about all the time . . .

– Until they see someone not moving.

And then you get the ones who are trying to *make* you move.

– Prodding and poking.

'I can see you breathing!'

– Waving selfie sticks in your face.

Getting up on the stand with you.

– Same reason. Can't bear the tension.

And they hate us for it, for making them feel bad.

Sh . . . More of them.

*

Nothing?

– Nothing.

I sometimes just long to let go. Blink. Have a twitch.

– I'm all right as long as no one talks about it . . .

I wouldn't mind having a quick twitch right now.

– Me, too, but just don't say it!

Left cheek. Huge twitch struggling to get out. It's driving me crazy.

– I'm not listening.

Just one twitch . . . No one's going to notice one little twitch . . .

– If I do one twitch I'll do two, and if I do two I'll never stop.

I can't hold out any longer . . .

– Listen! Another lot . . .

*

– 10p. And after I managed not to twitch! I thought I heard paper money in yours.

Old toffee-apple wrapper.

– Oh, no! Unbelievable, some of these bastards!

In the tin, that was. In my hand . . .

– Not the old toffee-apple?

Half-eaten.

– What did you do?

Nothing.

– Not even twitch?

Not even blink.

– So you're what – still holding it?

Tea-break in two hours' time. I'll get rid of it then.

– Never mind. Better to be living statues.

Better than what?

– Dead ones.

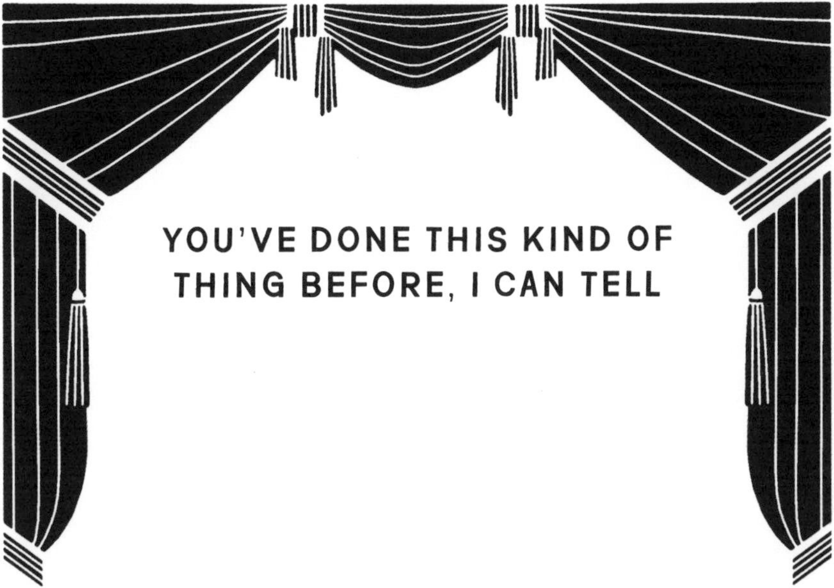
YOU'VE DONE THIS KIND OF
THING BEFORE, I CAN TELL

Simon Spout, in the course of your long and successful career you have been interviewed many times. I've checked the cuttings, and my best estimate is that the interview which you are kindly giving me today is your eight-hundred-and-seventy-first. At least 233 of these interviews I have conducted myself.

So, Simon – as I hope I may call you after all these years! – or Sir Simon, as you have become somewhere along the way! – my first question is this:

I can't help noticing that you have been asked the same questions many times – by me among others – and, occasional lapses of memory apart, have given the same answers. I take it that you don't expect me to have thought of anything new to ask you this time, and that you're not planning to say anything new in reply, if indeed there is anything new left to be said . . . Wait, wait! I haven't got there yet!

I know, too, how fed up you are with being interviewed, because you've said so in previous interviews many times. And you can guess how fed up I am with interviewing you. I'm not sure why either of us is doing it yet again, except to provide us both with some written confirmation of our own existence.

Not that anyone except perhaps you and my elderly Auntie Florence is going to read the results . . .

Wait, wait! You keep jumping in before I've finished! You'll know when I've got to the end of the question because there'll be a question mark. Hanging in the air between us. An upward inflection of the voice. Followed by a pause for your answer.

Where was I . . . ? Ignore that question mark!

Yes. You and my elderly Auntie Florence – who will soon be too
demented to read interviews, which will halve our audience. So, Simon.
Or Sir Simon, if I may. To speed things up and make this interview as
painless as possible for both of us I'm going to put my questions to you in
multiple choice form. Are you happy with this? Yes/no . . . ?

Yes? Yes. Thank you. And since you may not remember what answer
you gave when I asked you a question before, I'll simply look up your
previous answer, and assume that it's the same again unless you protest,
or for that matter even if you do.

All right? No need to answer that! Off we go, then.

Are you an optimist or a pessimist? Do you believe in a deity?
Is mankind doomed? What am I doing with my life? Why am I
interviewing you instead of you interviewing me, when I'm obviously

so much cleverer than you, and so much better informed about even your own work . . . ?

I beg your pardon? You said something. Did anyone ask you to open your mouth? *I* did? Not that I'm aware of. But, please, if you want to sound off about something, go right ahead. It's a free country . . . What . . . ?

In the bath? What do you mean, in the bath? That's the answer to a totally different question! Which I haven't asked! Would I ever ask anything as totally banal as 'Where do you get your ideas?'

You're still mumbling away about something . . . 'From nine to five'? Are you implying that I have asked you whether you work regular hours or only when you're inspired? My God, to make such an accusation after all these years together!

But I believe you have a story you want to tell me? One which you have told many times already, to many interviewers. Only seven times, though, to me personally, which is maybe why I've completely forgotten what it was . . .

No! Don't start telling me it now! I'll find it in the cuttings! In any case we've already moved on to the next question, which is: Why have you closed your eyes? Is it in order to concentrate on the interview? Or to indicate that it's over? Or because you have slipped into unconsciousness?

Or are in fact already dead . . . ?

No answer . . .

Hell's teeth! I'm going to have to rewrite this whole thing as an obit . . .

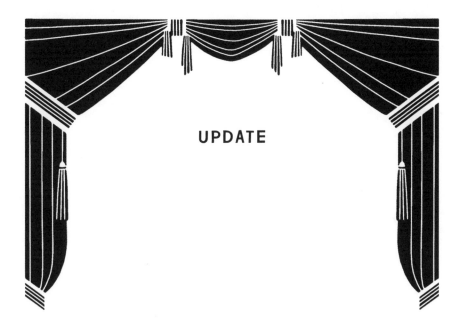

UPDATE

A new version of *Pocket Playhouse* is available.

This fixes a possible problem introduced by the last update, the one that was designed to fix the various problems arising from earlier updates. It also addresses difficulties that some readers have reported in remembering why in heaven's name they ever bought *Pocket Playhouse* in the first place.

Please choose between the following options:

Install – cheerfully, grateful for our continuing care
Install – reluctantly, complaining that the problem should have been fixed before *Pocket Playhouse* was ever put on the market

Terms and Conditions: A lot of small print follows which you needn't bother your head about, because no one ever does, and which merely says, if you really want to know, that you waive all your legal rights, and appoint Pocket Playhouse to be sole arbiter of any dispute that may arise, and also, while we're about it, to have an irrevocable power of attorney over your entire estate.

Agree
Disagree – of course, but what can I do?

Downloading . . . This will take up a surprising amount of your time and most of your remaining patience.

Reading files . . . Verifying . . . Processing . . . Rereading the more interesting files . . . Rewriting . . . Re-editing . . . Having a bit of a lie-down to recover . . .

Done! Please enter your *Pocket Playhouse* password to continue:

Your password! Yes? In the little box thing above! Come on . . .

You haven't forgotten it . . . ? Oh, no! Not again!

Hint: you wrote it down on the back of an envelope, which may still be behind the clock with various bills you've forgotten to pay . . .

Please have another try . . .

Hint: Not the make of your first car, or your mother's maiden name, or the name of that fluffy toy dog you had as a child, all of which are already known to internet crime syndicates around the world, and are on sale to anyone for under a pound . . .

No . . . No . . . No . . . Nothing like it . . . No . . .

Oh dear. This is getting very tedious.

Do *we* know it, here at Pocket Playhouse? Yes, of course we do, we know
everything about you, including your shoe size and your cholesterol level
(for which, incidentally, we suggest you should seek urgent professional
advice). Your password is right here in front of us, but we're not going
to tell you what it is, obviously, in case it's not you who's asking, but
someone merely pretending to be you, though why anyone should want
to pretend to be someone as useless as you are it's difficult to imagine.

And no, it's certainly not 'Damn and blast this whole bloody enterprise
and everyone involved in it.'

Please have one last try . . .

Come on, come on! Anything! The first word that comes into your head
. . . ! Just be aware, though, that if this one also fails the entire text will
without further warning suddenly and irretrieva

YOUR PRAYERS ANSWERED

Good morning, and welcome to My prayer-answering service! Please be aware that prayers may be recorded for training purposes.

In the current difficult world situation I am experiencing a high volume of traffic. You may wish to call back at a less fraught moment in the world's history.

For fire, police, or ambulance you may find it quicker to call your local emergency services. Minor sins, up to and including Anger, can usually be more quickly dealt with at parish level. For Gluttony, please contact your nearest obesity clinic. For Lust, please hold . . .

Your prayer has been placed in a queue. It will be answered by one of My Persons as soon as possible. Thank you for your patience.

While you are waiting, in order to give you the best possible service, I need to ask you a few simple questions.

Firstly, is this a private call, or are you a member of some organisation that prays professionally? If the latter, are you proposing to utter your prayer in some special ecclesiastical voice? If so I will transfer you to an operator who is trained to understand this particular dialect . . .

Thank you. You are making a private call. How long have you been a subscriber to this service? If you have a touch-tone phone, press one for 'All my life,' two for 'Since yesterday, when I discovered a strange lump in my armpit,' or three for 'Since two seconds ago, when I looked out of the window of the plane and saw flames coming out of the starboard outer engine . . .'

Thank you. You are a regular subscriber. Please choose carefully between the following options. Do you wish to talk to Me about:

1. The health and well-being of the sovereign?
2. The outcome of a forthcoming sporting event?
3. Problems with domestic appliances? If it's your computer please hold while I transfer your call to My seven-year-old granddaughter.
4. The shortcomings of your partner/aged parents/adolescent children?
5. Dissatisfaction with My meteorological or geological arrangements?
6. My own attributes . . . ?

Thank you. You have chosen to talk to Me about my own attributes. Please hold. One of My Persons will be with you shortly . . .

*

Hello there! I'm sorry you've had to wait. Thank you for your patience and understanding.

You have chosen to pray to me about my own attributes. If you wish to discuss my omnipotence, please press one. For my omniscience, press two. If it's my general benevolence you wish to congratulate me on, that's three. Alternatively, speaking clearly and simply, please tell me which of my other attributes it is that you most appreciate . . .

Thank you. Did you say that you were praising me for My gravy, though it's rather ruined your dress . . . ?

Thank you. You have praised me for My favour, To your fathers in distress. Is there anything else I can help you with today . . . ?

Thank you. You have also chosen to consult me about a personal problem . . .

Thank you. Did you say that you have had sexual relations with three Antarctic drinking horns . . . ?

Thank you. You have several relations coming to tea who aren't on speaking terms. Please check my website, where you will find a list of easy-to-bake recipes for the tea-table which are bound to be a talking-point for even the most difficult guests!

Before you go, please tell me your name and address, so that I can keep you up to date with all My exciting new offers . . .

Thank you. Did you say you are the seedy old dodderer at The Moorings, Oakdene Avenue, Carshalton Beeches . . . ?

Thank you. You are C. D. O'Donovan. And is the Moorings that house four doors along from the corner, with a blue front door and defective guttering . . . ?

Thank you. I did actually know, of course. I was just checking to make sure that this wasn't some kind of scam. Though if it had been I should of course have known!

Thank you for choosing to pray to Me today. It's been a pleasure listening to you.

And I should get that lump in your armpit checked rather urgently, if I were you.

CHE SARA

. . . and Act One of the opera draws to its close as Adalina, ordered
by her father Umberto to marry Anselmo, declares her undying love
for Rodolfo, the son of Umberto's sworn enemy Roberto, and brother
of Anselmo's beloved Serafina. Adalina's maid Giovanna, disguised
as Raimondo, page to Roberto, can only look on in bewilderment as
the voices of Adalina and Rodolfo, now joined by Roberto, Serafina,
Umberto, and Alfonso, blend in the famous *'Perchè o perchè'* – 'Why, oh
why, is everything thus and so? Whither is it all going, and how did we
come to get involved in it?'

When the curtain rises again for Act Two, in this live broadcast from
the Royal Opera House, Covent Garden, of Bellinzini's opera *Rodolfo*,
the scene will have shifted from Sicily to the Scottish Highlands. During
the interval Adalina's father, the Count of Pastasciutta, has formed an
alliance with his former enemy the Marchese di Renfrewshire . . .

Hold on a moment . . . What . . . ? Oh, right . . .

Apparently some listener in Nantwich has just tweeted the BBC website to ask how long this synopsis of the plot is going to go on. A very fair question, to which I can give you a very simple answer. It's going to go on until I reach the end of the story. All right?

Where was I? Oh, yes. Adalina's father. Alliance with the Duca di Ross e Cromarty. So, Rodolfo now enters disguised as Basilio . . .

Another tweet from Nantwich . . . 'Who is Basilio?' – I was in fact just about to explain!

Oh God, I hate all this interactive stuff you have to do nowadays . . . !

What . . . ? Yes, it *will* be midnight before I've finished if you don't let me get on with it! I'm going as fast as I can! There's a lot of plot here, and you can't see the surtitles in Nantwich . . . !

No, you won't miss anything, because they can't start until I've finished! I've got a little button here, and until the conductor gets the signal he's going to stay right where he is in the green room, watching the Test Match. So, if you want actually to hear some music, you'll have to be patient . . . !

You think you know it all up there in Nantwich, don't you. Well, let me tell you – you have no idea how complicated human relations can be! Jealousy! Revenge! Self-sacrifice! Cross-dressing! You know all about that kind of thing in *Nantwich*, do you? I don't think so, my friend. Not in *Nantwich*.

So, Rodolfo enters disguised as Clorinda . . .

Now what . . . ? A listener in Dunfermline . . . 'Who's Clorinda?' You mean you weren't listening when I explained about Clorinda . . . ? Yes, I did explain! Less than twenty minutes ago! Have I got to set you tests at the end of each act to make sure you're still with us? I know people's attention span is getting shorter and shorter these days, but this is ridiculous . . .

So, where were we . . . ? OK. Clorinda enters disguised as Rodolfo . . .

Who's *Rodolfo*? You don't know who *Rodolfo* is? He's only the one the whole opera's about, darling! He's only the title!

Never mind. I'll explain it all again. So – back to page one of the script . . . Only now I haven't got page one . . . I put it on the edge of the box here . . . It's gone . . .

So, from memory, Rodolfo is . . . well, he's Rodolfo. OK? You don't want his family tree, do you? You don't want his complete entry in *Who's Who* . . . ? No, I don't know what he does for a living! Writes opera synopses, probably . . .

Exactly – he has private means. His father owns half of Tuscany . . . Yes, Umberto also has private means . . . They all have private means.

Hold on . . . It's down there in the stalls. I can see it . . . Excuse me! *Excuse me* . . . ! Yes, me, up here, the one waving . . . ! That bit of paper you're holding – just take a look at it, will you, and remind me where Rodolfo went to school . . .

THIS IS THE TITLE OF THE
NEXT PIECE, THOUGH YOU MAY
NOT HAVE IMMEDIATELY
RECOGNISED IT AS A TITLE,
IN SPITE OF THE FACT THAT IT'S
IN BOLD CAPS AND CENTRED,
BECAUSE IT'S NOT SHORT
AND SNAPPY, LIKE ALL THE OTHER
TITLES YOU'VE SEEN,

AND IT'S NOT SHORT AND SNAPPY BECAUSE
WE TITLES ARE FED UP WITH BEING SHORT
AND SNAPPY, WHY SHOULD WE BE SUBJECT
TO SUCH UNFAIR RESTRICTIONS, WHEN THE
BODY TEXT, WHICH NOBODY WOULD READ
IF WE HADN'T STOOD UP HERE IN 28 POINT
CAPS AND CAUGHT PEOPLE'S INTEREST, IS
ALLOWED TO RAMBLE ON FOR AS LONG AS IT
LIKES, WHICH IS SURELY TOTALLY UNJUST,
WHY SHOULD TITLES NOT BE ALLOWED
FULL AND FREE EXPRESSION JUST LIKE
EVERY OTHER FORM OF COMMUNICATION,
EVEN MODERN POETRY, AND IF YOU THINK
THERE'S SOMETHING STRANGE ABOUT THE
SYNTAX THERE'S A REASON FOR THAT – IT'S

BECAUSE WE'RE NOT ALLOWED TO HAVE ANY FULL STOPS, WHICH IS BECOMING RIDICULOUS WHEN YOU GET TO SOMEWHERE AROUND HERE, AND WE'VE STILL GOT A LOT WE WANT TO SAY, INCLUDING WHY, IF WE'RE TITLES, WE'RE NOT LISTED IN THE NEW YEAR HONOURS LIST LIKE OTHER TITLES SUCH AS SIR AND LORD, IS IT BECAUSE WE HAVEN'T CONTRIBUTED TO THE FUNDS OF ANY POLITICAL PARTY, OR PERFORMED SOME OBSCURE FUNCTION IN THE ROYAL HOUSEHOLD, WHICH IS A QUESTION, AND MEANS THAT BY SOME CURIOUS ANOMALY, EVEN THOUGH WE ARE FORBIDDEN FULL STOPS, WE CAN END ON A QUESTION MARK?

Of course! Now it all comes bursting out! We down here in the Text of the piece itself always suspected that there was a lot of resentment concealed up there in the Title. That's probably why it's called the Title – because it has a sense of entitlement. It tries to look cool and laconic, but that's just a front to conceal its inadequacies. The next thing it'll be wanting is not just full stops, which is ridiculous enough, but also paragraph breaks, like this . . .

And even chapter headings. We'll enjoy one now, while the Title can only watch in impotent envy . . .

CHAPTER TWO

Why should the Text enjoy these privileges? cries the Title. Because we have earned them by having to be so long – while up there in the Title all they've ever done is to mumble two or three words that no one ever notices, in spite of all that straining to seem catchy and smart, and being indulged with the preposterously self-aggrandising accoutrements of capital letters and bold type. **WELL, TWO CAN PLAY AT THAT GAME – AND IF THE TITLE THINKS IT CAN RAMBLE ON FOR AS LONG AS IT LIKES THEN THE TEXT CAN RETALIATE BY STOPPING DISCONCERTINGLY SHORT, AND BRINGING THE WHOLE ENTERPRISE TO AN UNFEASIBLY PREMATURE CONCLUSION – WITHOUT EVEN THE BENEFIT OF A FULL STOP**

MASTERPROMPT

How do you learn your lines?

That's the first thing people always ask actors. How do you remember all those words? Page after page! Even if it's very boring. Or totally meaningless!

Well, I'm going to let you into a little professional secret. We don't!

Not these days! No more drudgery with words and lines! Thanks to MasterPrompt, the modern electronic technology that literally puts words into your mouth!

You think I had to learn all this stuff I'm saying now? I didn't! You think I'm standing here struggling to remember it? I'm not! I'm not even thinking about it! I'm thinking about supper. Whether to risk that pastrami-and-prune lasagne at the back of the fridge that's five days past its sell-by date . . . Also trying to remember whether it's Wednesday or Thursday, because if it's Thursday I forgot to put the recycling out . . .

So, yes, MasterPrompt! How does it work? Simple! I have a chip implanted under my skin, just here, behind my left ear, and the words are fed to me through the mobile phone network from a central server in Leamington Spa. All I have to do is open my mouth and let them out. And of course try to look as if I'm actually meaning them!

Or have I eaten it already . . . ? The lasagne. Sorry. Mind wandering. I really need MasterPrompt to start a new service thinking the thoughts I'm thinking while I'm not thinking about what I'm saying.

So what about stage directions? Can MasterPrompt do stage directions?

It certainly can! I never have to think about them! I just find myself . . .
laughing . . . crying . . . moving stage left . . .

And now I'm . . . what . . . ? I'm *chlschltchlshtlschmn* . . . Sorry – I'm
breaking up. Dead spot there. Try stage right . . .

So that's two prawn vindaloos, extra hot, with ketchup and French fries
. . . Sorry! You get a bit of interference sometimes . . .

All right, so what I'm doing now is . . . I'm taking my trousers off . . . ?
No – sorry – crossed line – some other theatre! What I'm doing is
explaining about the philosophical issues involved.

Because people say, 'But what about free will? Aren't you worried
about not having free will any more?' But I *have* got free will! Of course
I have! I don't have to open my mouth and let the words out if I don't

want to! I can simply keep it closed! Like this . . .

No – I can't keep it closed! It's opening of its own accord! It's saying these words!

I *can* keep it closed!

I can't keep it closed . . .

I *will* keep it closed!

I *won't* keep it closed . . .

But I *want* to keep it closed!

I *don't* want to keep it closed . . .

Listen, who's in charge here? Me or some faceless operative in Leamington Spa . . . ? What . . . ? The faceless operative in Leamington Spa *is* me . . . ?

But if I tell myself to . . . I don't know . . . take myself by the ear and lead myself round the stage, say, I'm obviously not going to do it . . . !

Oh, my God! I *am* going to! Agh! You bastard! *I* bastard! Let myself go . . . ! Thank you. Only playing! Oh, was I?

Look, I am actually a little embarrassed by this performance.

No, I'm not. *I'll* tell me when I'm embarrassed. *I'm* going to get right back to selling them the product. Yes, because you, too, can share my little secret! Let MasterPrompt put words into *your* mouth! Switch on, switch off, and think about Christmas! You do the happy smile,

MasterPrompt does the rest! When MasterPrompt's on the book, you're off the hook!

And if they don't like the result up there in Leamington Spa, then even halfway through your big number you can find yourself taking yourself by the ear-lobe for real . . . Agh . . . ! And propelling yourself off . . . Just like I'm doing now . . . And giving yourself your own Acas-compliant dismissal letter!

Have a wonderful day!

REMEMBERING REMEMBERED

Darling, you remember you asked me about that man we met at that thing we went to?

    – No? What man? What thing?

Darling, we had a long conversation about him!

    – Did we? What did we say?

I don't remember what we actually *said*. But you must remember that we did have a conversation!

    – Hold on. Is this going to be another one?

Another one of what?

    – Another conversation about not remembering things?

Why – have we had conversations before about not remembering things?

– What do you mean? We *keep* having them!

Do we?

– There was that one on page 19 for a start. You don't remember that?

Page 19? When were we ever on page 19?

– Immediately after page 18!

You mean that page just before page 20?

– Oh, so you remember page 20?

Why, what happened on page 20?

– I've no idea. Except it came after page 19. And we had another one on page 115.

I do remember that one. Only it wasn't us. Was it?

– Wasn't us? What do you mean, it wasn't us?

Having the conversation. I think it was some other couple. That's probably why I remember it.

– Darling! You must remember whether it was us or not!

Not necessarily. I've got a lot of other things to remember. So *was* it us?

– Yes! Us! And now we're having another conversation! Yes? You and me! Not some other couple! You haven't forgotten that yet?

Not yet, no. So we keep having these conversations, do we?

– We do.

About not remembering things?

– About not remembering tbings.

Then that's why I don't remember them. Because we keep having them. If it was just one conversation I'd remember it. Like getting married.

   – Oh, you remember getting married? And you remember it was me you married, not someone else?

Yes, because it didn't *keep* happening. But if I *kept* getting married, then it would be like remembering taking my pills each morning, and I *wouldn't* remember.

   – You don't remember taking your pills?

Not every separate instance of taking them, no. Not taking them last Friday, say. Not on October 17th last year.

   – But this morning, at any rate?

Yes, of course . . . Except – 'Wednesday'! Isn't it Wednesday today? Here they are, look, still in the 'Wednesday' slot!

– Maybe you took Tuesday's today, because you forgot yesterday . . .

Or Monday's on Tuesday, because I forgot Monday . . .

– At least you remember it was you who forgot and not me.

I'd better take them now before I do . . .

LOOKING BACK

Honestly, some of the people you get coming into an art gallery these days! Look at them! A four-year-old child could do better than that!

– Sh, darling! They'll hear you!

Let them. *We're* not supposed to mind if we hear what they're saying about us.

– They don't realise we *can* hear.

No, just because we're hanging up here on the wall in a gilt frame with a sign saying we're painted by Gainsborough they think we're deaf. And blind. They think we can't see the way they look at us and their eyes glaze over, and then they yawn and look at their watch.

– What I don't like is the ones who come and put their face up so close to you that the alarm goes off. It always makes me jump.

I hate the ones who keep going on about our being painted by Gainsborough. 'Oh, look, it's a Gainsborough!' That's all they care about – that we were painted by Gainsborough. It would be nice if occasionally someone said, 'Oh, look, it's Mr and Mrs Andrews!'

– Be fair, darling. We don't peer at them and say, 'Oh, look, it's Mr and Mrs Splotchett!'

No, because we don't know their names! And why don't we know their names? Because they haven't had the common courtesy to step into a frame with a sign on it! They haven't bothered to get themselves listed in the catalogue! But we certainly don't peer at them and say, 'Oh, look, it's a God!' Or 'Oh, look, this one was done by her father and mother! What an interesting example of sexual reproduction!'

– Do keep your voice down, darling.

I am keeping my voice down. Look at this one, though. The one who's peering so closely at the brushwork on my trousers. Have you ever seen a portrait that looks like that! *You* don't look like that!

– Of course not. I'm a work of art. But, darling, life doesn't have to be artlike!

God knows, I don't expect photographic realism. But life has to say *something* about art! These people are so three-dimensional. You and I don't bulge out backwards and forwards in space in that ridiculous way. You can't believe these creatures are supposed to represent real figures of paint and canvas.

– Darling, just because you and I are flat doesn't mean that everything has to be.

But they keep moving around all the time! They keep waving their arms about and pulling faces! It's so kitschy! Like something you see on television.

– Actually I think this couple's quite interesting. Look at his stomach. You can see the influence of Rubens very clearly. And she's pure Giacometti. Also the iconology of her trousers is very significant. The knees being ripped like that. It tells you something about her.

Tells you what about her?

– Well, that she's devout. That she spends a lot of her time praying.

I know you did a module about this kind of thing at that finishing school you went to. But what are these people supposed to *mean*?

– They don't *mean* anything! They're just – people. Abstract shapes.

They're not the kind of thing you'd want in your living room, though, are they. Moving about and bumping into things. Yawning and grinning. Bulging away all over the place.

– But we can't only have the Arnolfinis round all the time, darling. They do get a bit boring, you know, just standing there holding hands and not saying anything.

Well, at least the Arnolfinis don't *bulge*.

THE CORRECTED VERSION

In the beginning I created the heaven and the earth. And the earth was without form and void . . .

– It was absolute chaos! You've never seen anything like it . . . ! Oh, sorry, Darling . . . ! My Husband hates being interrupted when He's telling a story . . . ! Go on, Darling – I won't say another word.

And darkness was upon the face of the deep . . .

– Pitch dark! You couldn't see a hand in front of you, even if there had been any hands to see! Sorry . . .

And My spirit moved upon the face of the waters . . .

– Yes, He somehow found this wonderful spirit who came in and set to work, moving upon the face of the waters and so on. Such a treasure! Really rolled up his sleeves. No tea-breaks! Cleaned up as he went along! If you ever need a spirit do let me know.

And I said, Let there be light . . .

– And there *was* light! Just like that! No waiting to be connected, no filling up of forms. Just – 'Let there be light.' As soon as people know it's My Husband they can't do enough for Him. Now, that was on the Monday. Or was it Tuesday by that time? It was the day We put the recycling out, I know that . . . No, it was the Monday, it must have been, because on the Tuesday My Husband said . . .

Let there be a firmament . . .

– 'Let there be a firmament,' and I said, oh, I don't know, I'm not sure I want a firmament – because I didn't actually know what a firmament was! – but He never takes any notice of anything *I* say, so He just went ahead and put it there . . .

In the midst of the waters . . .

– In the midst of the waters, and He was absolutely right, as usual, because it looks divine – you must come and see it, it's reflected in the waters. And anyway, then He laid the lawn, and planted trees.

And the evening and the morning were the second day.

– The third day, Darling!

The second day.

– Darling, it was the Wednesday when you did the grass and the flowers and all the rest of it! He always gets this bit muddled up. Flowers don't mean anything to Him, that's the trouble. He just lumps everything in together.

And the evening and the morning were the third day . . .

– Exactly. Thank you. I hate contradicting, but Mr Moses is writing all this down for posterity and We do want to get it right.

And I made two great lights . . .

– The sun and the moon, but You need to explain that, Darling, or people will think You mean You put some terrible carriage-lamp things outside the front door.

. . . the stars also . . .

– And of course He *hasn't* stopped to explain, He's just gone charging on regardless.

. . . and I saw that it was good.

– You saw it was good, yes, but if You talk at the same time as me, Darling, Mr Moses can't hear what you're saying . . . But on He goes! Where have we got to now?

. . . Great whales . . .

– Oh, whales, yes – Friday.

. . . winged fowls . . .

– Birds! Some with the most beautiful plumage, but of course they started to eat the raspberries.

. . . and creeping things . . .

– Yes, some horrible creepy-crawlies, but I didn't like to say anything because He hates being criticised.

. . . So I created man in My Own image . . .

– Yes, it was Saturday by this time, and He created this little man to look after everything, and have dominion over it all, and so on, and his name's Adam, and he's a bit simple, and also a nudist, which was rather a shock, but I said fine, I'll just pretend not to notice.

And I saw every thing that I had made, and behold, it was very good . . .

– And it was! I have to admit that! It was utterly perfect! The whole garden – absolutely divine! If only you'd come and seen it that weekend! But, oh dear – all too good to be true! Because the *following* week . . . Perhaps I shouldn't tell you this, because if you ask Him He'll tell you He made her simply to help Adam in the garden, but honestly, as soon as I saw her standing there, *also* without a stitch on, I said, No, my Darling, naked *women* – no, absolutely not! And He's going to tell you some story about a . . .

. . . serpent . . .

. . . a serpent, well, fine, and if you believe that you'll believe anything, but the long and short of it is that she's gone, and she's taken the gardener with her, so if you know of anyone, not a woman, thank you, and preferably not a nudist . . .

HELL'S KITCHEN

– the unique new total dining experience!

Have you ever gone to some highly recommended restaurant and been disappointed to find the background music not quite all-pervasive enough to stop you hearing what you and your fellow-diners were saying? That left you still able to think? Even to taste the food you were eating?

At Hell's Kitchen all this is a thing of the past!

Our philosophy:
You know from TV that *haute cuisine* requires noise and bullying, burns and burnout.

At Hell's Kitchen we believe that eating *haute cuisine* is no less demanding. Our kitchens are hell, certainly – but so is our dining room!

Our chefs' lives are a misery – and we do our damnedest to make our customers' lives no less horrible!

We know that however highly amplified the background music may be in traditional restaurants, its effect is often weakened by distracting traces of harmony – even of melody. Intrusive tunes and voices make it difficult to enjoy the pure grinding insistence of the bass.

At Hell's Kitchen we promise you: no artificial ingredients! No guitars, no keyboards, no drums, no synthesisers! Nothing but real natural sounds, produced organically by trusted suppliers on a fascinating variety of genuine industrial machines!

No tunes! No chords! No words! Just –

Thump, thump, thump! Thump-thumpetty-thump! Boom, boom, boom!

Woomph-woomphetty-woomph!

The result? – The ideal background for relaxed conversation! You can't hear what anyone else is saying – *they* can't hear what *you're* saying! Just sit back and read whatever you like into your fellow-diners' inaudible mouthing! Wit and wisdom! Mutually advantageous business offers! Proposals of marriage! Exciting rows . . . ! The choice is yours!

> *– All our waiting staff are certified as having at least*
> *50 per cent hearing loss. –*

SAMPLE MENU

Entrée:
A feuilleté of pneumatic drill, served in bite-sized three-minute
bursts on a bed of lightly sprayed asphalt, matured concrete,
and robust roadstone.

Main course:
Traditional English Pile-driver. Fifty-year-old recovered
Middlesbrough steel, richly robed in a sauce of phosphate rust-
proofing, served as a leisurely series of spine-jarring impacts on
a coulis of London clay and a crunchy crumble of palaeozoic
rock.

Dessert:
The Hell's Kitchen Steel Plate. An irresistible international
medley of riveting from shipyards around the world.

<u>*OUR GOURMET MENU*</u> *(supplementary prices apply)*

A range of completely continuous background sounds specially
selected to satisfy the particularly demanding diner who finds
that even the quieter intervals between thumps detract from
his gastronomic pleasure.

Amuse-gueule:
Garden salad – Strimmer with leaf blower topping.

Entrée:
Printer's Pie – A Grausam & Taubmacher newspaper press
running at 110 decibels to produce a luscious redtop studded
with tasty nuggets of home-cooked celebrity gossip.

Main course:
Thai and Die – A fully-laden British Airways Boeing 747
bound for Bangkok starting its take-off run at Heathrow
(North Runway, air temperature 18 degrees, wind SSW 19 kph
gusting to 29 kph).

Dessert:
Délice écossaise – A London–Edinburgh express passing
through Grantham Station at 120 mph.

Digestif:
The *maître de l'enfer* recommends a delicate 50s vintage of carefully manicured fingernails being scraped down a lightly chalk-dusted blackboard with overtones of calculus and classical Greek.

– A selection of popular headache pills is offered as a courtesy to our patrons at no extra cost. –

– Also food. –

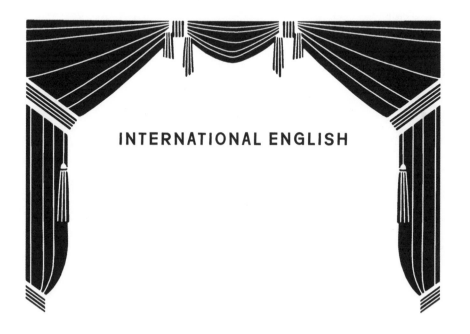

INTERNATIONAL ENGLISH

Hi! You're Ecuador, right? Anyone sitting here?

– No, please, take a seat. And you're . . . ?

Moldova.

– Moldova, yes, I can see your badge.

I just wanted, if I may be personal for a moment, to place on record how highly I appreciated the contribution you made today in the Working Group on Gender Stereotyping in Indefinite Pronouns . . .

– Oh, thank you. That's very positive and constructive of you.

You really communicated! Some of those guys in there, they come to a conference like this on international communication, and they can't so little as raise a point of order in accepted international English.

– I know! What do they want – we should all speak Latvian?

So how come you're sitting out here in the lobby, and you're not in the six o'clock session on Functional Trans-lingual Standardisation of the Subjunctive?

– Phone. I had to take an urgent call from my husband in Quito.

Oh, your husband, right.

– He wanted as a matter of urgency to initiate a wide-ranging discussion of the conceptual and methodological framework of marriage in a changing society, with particular reference to women playing a non-traditional role in modern conference-going. And you? How come you're also sitting out here in the lobby?

My wife.

– Your wife. Of course.

She is making a nuanced reappraisal of disaggregated data with respect to our marriage, with the long-term aim of facilitating the mitigation of underlying systemic weakness.

– So this could be a useful opportunity for the two of us here to constitute ourselves an informal study group for the evening . . .

. . . tasked with examining the whole question of intra-organisational communication, and looking at ways of harmonising in-house personal relationships so as to meet a broad spectrum of individual needs without loss of functionality.

– I therefore propose we should take this forward by initiating round-table talks, within the overarching framework of the relevant procedural constraints, with a remit to adopt a constructive approach to establishing guidelines for setting up a workshop which would serve as a forum for a fruitful person-to-person dialogue . . .

Hey, Ecuador, your international English! Did anyone ever tell you how beautiful it is?

– Thank you. I do try firmly to orient the priority axis of my English towards the implementation of an agenda for significant positive action.

Me, too! With, as a long-term strategic objective . . .

– . . . the drawing-up of a road map . . .

. . . combining enhanced resource efficiency with a regional integration process . . .

– . . . of broad-spectrum policy options for what we might on a basis of mutual agreement do in the next few hours!

Wow, Ecuador, we make music together!

– It is a matter of regret to me, though, that up to now we still haven't got the expression 'key players' in.

No – nor 'on a case-by-case basis'.

– Nevertheless, I believe that with sensitive mutual consultation to progress the programme we can action a robust initiative to get even formulations such as 'medium-term global solutions' on to the table.

As an urgent first imperative I suggest implementing with immediate effect an adjournment to a closed session . . .

– in a mutually agreed secure venue . . .

. . . and, given the increasing strength of bilateral feeling which I believe is evident here, I believe we should prioritise a speedy resolution . . .

– . . . by posing the crucial question in stark and simple terms . . .

. . . that make crystal clear its relevance to us as ordinary conference-goers in the world today.

– In other words . . .

. . . my place or yours?

QUEST

Hello! I have journeyed here to Tierra del Fuego, at the ends of the earth, in search of one of history's most elusive characters.

Past these desolate, storm-wracked coasts sailed Ferdinand Magellan, nearly six hundred years ago, when he first circumnavigated the earth, and, half a century later, Sir Francis Drake, the buccaneering adventurer who famously stooped to finish his game of bowls, though not here in Tierra del Fuego. Countless brave men since then have left their bones in these turbulent waters.

But I have come here not in the footsteps of Magellan or Drake, or any of the other great mariners who passed this way.

I have come in search of T. J. Sprodd.

The nineteenth-century poet T. J. Sprodd is one of the unsolved mysteries of literary history. Sometimes known as the Nuneaton Nightingale, he seems to have left little trace outside a very small area of the West Midlands, and even the most diligent investigation on Wikipedia by this programme's team of researchers has been unable to trace any connection whatsoever with Tierra del Fuego.

But there's not much to film in Nuneaton, and there may possibly be in Tierra del Fuego. So I have come here, with nothing but a warm anorak, a change of underwear, a hundredweight of camera and lighting equipment, and a crew of twelve, to visit some of the more filmable locations that my advance team has found, and a few of the more photogenic locals who can speak a few words of English.

Journey with me, then, to meet some of the colourful local hairdressers, and drop in unannounced on the craftsmen who weave Tierra del

Fuego's traditional T-shirts, with their world-famous humorous logos. Whether we shall find any hitherto unsuspected descendants of the elusive Sprodd remains to be seen. But at least we shall have used up some of the air miles that the producers have accumulated over the years doing other programmes with a quest format.

From Tierra del Fuego the trail will lead us on to the steamy jungles of Borneo, which the director thinks will make a nice contrast with this awful place, though whether any of the shrunken heads we shall be looking at there ever belonged even to the most distant collateral branch of Sprodd's family seems unlikely. Then from Borneo I shall journey seven thousand miles further still – empty-handed, perhaps, with little to show from our stay in the jungle but any of a variety of possible parasitic infections – to Spitzbergen, in the Arctic Sea, another place that Sprodd almost certainly never visited, in the hope of finding some clue to the mystery, some distant trace of his existence, however faint – a poignantly mouldering picture postcard of Nuneaton, perhaps, left by some passing explorer, or a broken beer-mug of the sort that he may once have supped a thoughtful half of local ale from.

From Spitzbergen we shall journey on, by canoe and helicopter, by sledge and Underground train, to some place so remote, so little known, that neither I nor even our much-travelled location manager have yet been able to find it on the map.

And so, finally, in week twelve of the series, travel-stained and weary, I shall follow the trail all the way back to Nuneaton, where we shall probably arrive, after all our weeks and months on the road, to discover that a certain Mrs Cynthia Treadforth, the only witness we could find who had even so much as heard of Sprodd, and who had waited so patiently for her moment on camera, has just passed away.

Then on, on again, beyond even Nuneaton, this time by bus and bicycle, since I shall no longer be on expenses, in quest not of T. J. Sprodd, about whom my insatiable professional curiosity will perhaps by this time be after all very nearly sated, but of my own front door, and the 329 pints of milk standing in front of it that I suspect I forgot to cancel before I set out.

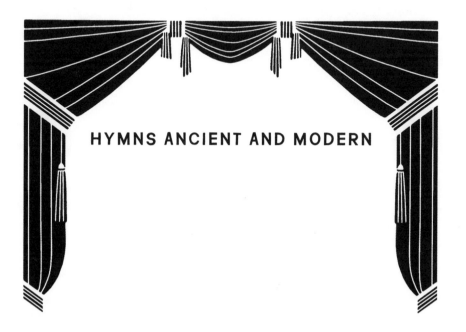

HYMNS ANCIENT AND MODERN

From the Morning Post, November 23rd, 1893

Cable and telegraph offices were overwhelmed last night by the flood of tributes pouring in from fans all over the world to the Reverend Francis Giffard Smith, the legendary creator of some of the best loved and most groundbreaking hymns of the nineteenth century, who died yesterday aged fifty-seven after a long battle with depression and incense addiction.

His 1861 hit 'God's Gas' was the first Church of England hymn to sell a million copies worldwide. Its words – 'Lord, fill us with Thy heaven'ly gas,/Like street-lights in the dark,/Then like the lamp-lighter supply/The municipal spark!' – spoke to people of all classes and none.

'He changed my life,' said Her Majesty the Queen in a statement issued from the Palace last night. 'It was hearing Smith performing some of the numbers from his 1871 Golden Hymnal Award-winning album *Hymns for Monarchs Young in Heart* that inspired me to reign on and give my name to an entire era.'

The Prime Minister, the Rt Hon. William Gladstone, told *The Times* newspaper: 'He was the voice of his generation. The influence of his music can be seen upon every corner of life in this country, from antimacassar design to parliamentary reform, from the development of new explosives to the improvement of urban sewerage.'

His Grace the Archbishop of Canterbury told the thousands of fans who had gathered outside Westminster Abbey: 'Without Smith the Victorian Age would never have become a byword for uncomplaining poverty, sanctimonious wealth, photogenic air pollution, and robust sexual hypocrisy.'

Composer Johannes Brahms cabled: 'He was the daddy of us all.'

Smith's Choral Evensongs were famous for their spectacle. In the course of the service he would appear out of a cloud of incense in a series of eye-popping mauve, crimson, and gold copes and chasubles, with the candlelight flashing around him from dozens of swinging silver thuribles. It was the unpredictability of his behaviour, though, that was perhaps most loved by the record crowds who fought for places in churches and cathedrals on his tours. He and his backing group once trashed an entire mediaeval rood screen. Smith, accompanying himself on the organ, would sometimes pound the keyboard to destruction, while screaming women worshippers threw their flannel drawers and whalebone corsets at him.

His early hymns were published by Grubhawk and Chimney, but, as his success grew, relations with the firm became strained, and he moved for a reported three-figure sum to Bagstraw and Strooth. The years that followed saw him produce some of his biggest hits, such as 'Thy Heavenly Glory' ('That raineth down,/Like hot brown Windsor soup') and 'Steam of Heaven' ('Full steam ahead we blindly race,/We surely must go smash!/Were not God's hands outstretched to save,/Like buffers for the crash.')

His tempestuous on-off relationship with glamorous hymnstress Mrs Cecil Chobb, who wrote some of the century's biggest hits for younger worshippers – 'Nor e'en a wagtail wags its tail/Save God hath told it to,' and 'We thank Thee, Lord, for whooping-cough' – produced endless column inches in Church of England fanzines. There were many other women in his life, from deaconesses to dignitaries of the Mothers' Union – and also suggestions of more eclectic tastes. He always denied reports of a clandestine relationship with the Bishop of Broadstairs, but it was often remarked that he had a habit of ending hymns with the words 'Ah, men!'

In time the incense took its toll, and his growing problems came to a head at a service to mark the Queen's Golden Jubilee in 1887, where he kept the congregation waiting for two hours, before appearing visibly the worse for holy smoke. The worshippers booed and catcalled, whereupon he ripped off his chasuble and showed them his naked underchasuble. It was shortly after this that he entered a priory suffering from nervous exhaustion. This was to be the first of many such retreats, and he later confessed to an ecclesiastical friend that he had very little memory of anything that had happened in those years.

In later life he became a recluse. A planned comeback tour never materialised, and he supported himself by writing suggestive songs for various lesser-known music-hall artists. Until the end, though, there always seemed to be young women prepared to wash his cassocks or swing a thurible or two with him.

He leaves an estimated seventeen children by various partners, his celebrated wardrobe of albs and surplices, and a vast acreage of gushing newsprint.

WHO AM I?

Oh, so you have finally deigned to pick up the phone, have you? Are you aware, young woman, that you have kept me waiting for nearly one and a quarter minutes? Do you know who I am . . . ?

I thought perhaps not. Let me tell you, then.

I am Lord Blastwater.

Blastwater, yes! B-L-A-S-T-W-A-T-E-R! *Lord* Blastwater! Lord Blastwater of Bludgerden, to be precise! Chairman of Associated Swill Industries!

And let me tell you something else, young woman. The Chairman of *your* company happens to be a business associate of mine, and he will be interested to learn that one of his employees has kept an important customer waiting for nearly one and a quarter minutes before she condescended to . . .

I beg your pardon? *Not* Lord Blastwater? What do you mean, I'm *not* Lord Blastwater . . . ?

Not that sort of person at all . . . ? Underneath? Deep down inside . . . ? My dear young woman, adding insolence to inefficiency is scarcely calculated to . . .

You know I'm really what . . . ? A sensitive and caring human being who longs only to reach out lovingly to others?

Sensitive, am I? Well, yes, if you mean sensitive to slackness and ill manners! Caring, certainly. Caring deeply about getting proper service and being treated with normal politeness and respect! And as for – what was it? – longing to reach out lovingly to others, then let me assure you that I already do all the reaching out that I wish to, thank you very much . . .

Well, to my employees among others . . . ! Yes, I have excellent relations with all of them. And please don't try to tell me that the loyalty and devotion of my chauffeur Carlos, for example, or my housekeeper Mrs Trudge, are merely the result of my paying them a little above the going rate . . .

Do they actually love me . . . ? Certainly they do . . . ! Not for myself alone, no, of course not! Partly for myself and partly for what I pay them. Which includes a substantial Christmas bonus, incidentally, not to mention of course their accommodation, which these days . . .

So I'm not *what* . . . ? In a meaningful relationship . . . ? This ridiculous modern jargon! No, I am not currently in a meaningful relationship, as it happens. Which is not to say that I have never been . . . !

When? In 1992 . . . Well, that was when it started. It ended in 1994 . . . Not at all – by mutual agreement . . . Exactly – when Lady Blastwater found out . . . And when did the marriage end? In 1995. I did my best to reanimate it, but . . . Exactly, exactly . . .

Distressed? Yes, I was. Heartbroken . . . Which is why I've learnt to be a little more careful since then in reaching out, as you put it, to other human beings . . .

Underneath, though . . . Exactly . . . Deep down inside . . . Of course . . .

Did I ever write poetry . . . ? Well, when I was a young man, yes, certainly . . . Oh, you know, the usual sort of stuff – love, nature . . .

I did have one volume published, yes, as it happens . . . Slim? Well, yes, I was, because this was before I was obliged to eat business lunches and City dinners . . . Oh, the book. Yes, the book was – well – certainly not corpulent . . .

The title? I told you – Blastwater. Blastwater of Bludgerden . . . Oh, of the book . . . I 've forgotten . . . Totally forgotten . . . You don't believe anyone could forget the title of their one book . . . ?

Well . . .

I take it you're not intending to make this conversation public in any way . . . ?

So, all right, it was *o mournful fires o sad desires* . . . No, I'm not going to say it again . . . All in lower case, yes . . .

Under the name 'Blastwater'? No, of course not! This was long before
I was graciously honoured by Her Majesty for my services to the waste
products industry. Before I even first set foot in swill . . . It was under my
name at the time . . .

I don't think it really matters what my name was . . . Well, it was Smeech
. . . *Smeech*, yes . . . C. B. Smeech . . . What do the initials stand for? The
B is for Bolderwood. Which was my mother's family name . . . When I
was a little boy my mother and I were very close . . . And when I think of
her now . . . Well, that's another story . . .

My middle name, yes. Originally . . . On the book? No, not on the book.
Not Bolderwood Smeech on the book . . .

C. B. Smeech? Well . . . Just C . . . No, not the bare initial. The name.
What the C stands for . . .

Ashamed of it? Certainly not . . .

No, it wasn't Cecil . . . Not Clarence . . . Not Claud . . .

Cedric, in fact, if you must know . . . Cedric Smeech, yes . . . *o mournful fires o sad desires* by Cedric Smeech.

Most kind of you, but I shouldn't bother searching the bookshops for it. I should imagine the only copies that still exist are the ones at the back of my bookcase . . . Behind the bound volumes of *Food Waste Reclamation International* . . . Oh, two or three hundred . . .

No – not at all. I've found the conversation rather interesting. I have in fact been pondering for some time now, in the way that people do as they get older, the whole question of who I really am. I catch sight of this stranger in the mirror. Bolderwood Blastwater. Who is he? Chairman of Associated Swill Industries, yes. Master of the Honourable Binmen's Company. But is that really me . . . ?

So, yes, I suppose you could say that I've been trying to *find myself* . . .

Where did I look? Well, in Davos, in Bermuda . . . *Did* I find myself? Not really, no . . .

Have I ever thought of looking where . . . ? In that old suitcase at the top of the cupboard? Which cupboard? You mean the one in the spare room . . . ? And you think . . . ? Well, it doesn't seem very likely, but . . .

Hold on, then . . . If you don't mind waiting for a few minutes . . .

*

Are you still there . . . ?

You're right! In the suitcase! Hidden under a lot of yellowing old draft accounts and company reports! Me! Cedric Smeech, scribbling away still in a leather-bound notebook my mother gave me on my sixteenth birthday!

Oh, I'm so pleased to see myself again! I thought I'd gone forever! I shed a few tears, I can tell you, when I saw myself lurking there!

I've *found myself* at last! After all these years! And it's all thanks to you! But, listen – I still don't know who *you* are . . .

Asphodel? *Asphodel* . . . That's a very pretty name. Were you always Asphodel . . . ? No? I thought not . . . ! Margaret . . . ? No, a very good move. Asphodel's much nicer. Much more *you*!

Now, listen, Asphodel. You may have given me back my inner Cedric Smeech, but if I'm going to go on earning a living I've still got to be Lord Blastwater of Bludgerden to the rest of the world! So, Asphodel, if one word of this conversation should ever be made public, let me warn you that in about two minutes flat you will find yourself holding your personal effects in a brown cardboard box, being escorted to the door of your office by security staff, and facing charges of making abusive telephone calls, sexual harassment, and using a false identity with intent to deceive.

Because that's me, Asphodel, the outer me, that one that really counts.

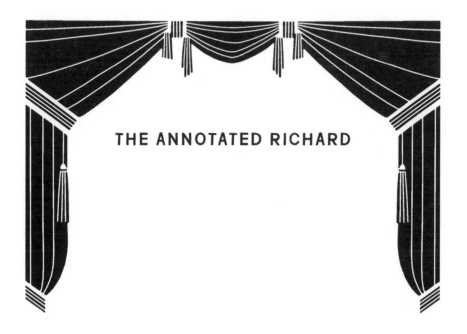

THE ANNOTATED RICHARD

GLOUCESTER:
Now is the winter of our discontent
Made glorious summer by this sun of York;
And all the clouds . . .

T. J. SPONG:
Your Grace!

GLOUCESTER:
. . . that lour'd upon our house . . .

T. J. SPONG:
If I might just break in here . . .

GLOUCESTER:
In the deep bosom of the ocean buried . . .

T. J. SPONG:

I do apologise for this, Your Grace!
I realise how maddening it is
To find yourself so rudely interrupted
Just as you first begin to hit your stride!
Oh, yes – I should explain: I'm Dr Spong,
The one who annotates the printed text.
And if the printed text needs explanation
Then how much more the version on the stage,
Where archaic words and strange obscure allusions
Go winging through the stalls like swerving swallows
Too fast and flickersome for us to grasp!
And so today's exciting innovation:
The living footnote for the live theatre!
The scholarly remark in real time!
So, please, Your Grace, go on! Soliloquise

As if I were not here! Where had we got to?

GLOUCESTER:
Now are our brows bound with victorious wreaths –

T. J. SPONG:
But can we first go back a line or two?
'This sun of York.' When spoken on the stage,
As here it is, it bears a double meaning!
As in that warming summer *sun* we hear
The *son*, the scion of the House of York.
Your Grace, I'm sure, perceived this for himself.
But what Your Grace may well not be aware of,
Since you were dead so long before this happened –
The fact that York itself, that noble city,
Became a most important railway centre!

JANE TROUNCER:

And also famous for producing chocolate,
A pleasure still in your day undiscovered!
– I'm Dr Trouncer, an authority
On one of Shakespeare's major unsolved riddles:
The total lack of toffees in his plays.
– Yes, had Your Grace but lived a little later,
And tasted Rowntree's Kit Kat . . .

SANDRA SMITH:

                              Or their Aero!
Oh, Sandra Smith – and not an English scholar! –
A simple girl who loves the open air –
Especially wrapped inside a chocolate bar!
And yes, had you but felt those subtle bubbles
So tickly-prickly bursting on thy tongue . . .

JANE TROUNCER:

Or seen the good Lord Rowntree's coloured Smarties
Come tumbling from their caskets like rich hail
Of rubies, emeralds, chalcedonies –
Luxuriant as the royal jewels you crave!

SANDRA SMITH:

It might have made your character more sweet
And changed the course of English history!

WALTER WELKIN:

Though, sadly, ruin'd the plot of Shakespeare's play –
The which, as Master of the Royal Scrolls
And Keeper of Renaissance Narrative,
I feel an obligation to preserve.

GLOUCESTER:

Now will I in, to take some privy order,
To draw the brats of Clarence out of sight . . .

PROFESSOR DOKTOR HELMUT BESSERWISS:

But first, if I may introduce myself:
Professor Doktor Helmut Besserwiss,
Director, Faculty of Anglistik,
The University of Schnorkelstein.
Please note: my name, my job, and my address –
Iambic all! And all pentameters!
My lifetime's task has been to make them so!

T. J. SPONG:

Your point, Herr Doktor Besserwiss?

PROFESSOR DOKTOR HELMUT BESSERWISS:
                    My point?
Why, none, save but to show how seriously
We take our Shakespeare here in Schnorkelstein!
A footnote to a footnote, nothing more!

WALTER WELKIN:
A footfootnote! And like the footnotesman
Himself . . .

JANE TROUNCER:
. . . or *her*self!

WALTER WELKIN:
. . . *her*self, certainly . . .
The footnoteperson . . . surely more secure

On two feet than on one! A balanced view!

WAYNE SCRUNGE:
'On one foot this, and on the other that.'
Such lame bipedalism's out of date!
Please see my paper in *Shakespearean Studies*,
In which I say quite brutally and bluntly –

KING RICHARD:
If I might interject one line at least –

WAYNE SCRUNGE:
Who's this, so rudely interrupting . . . ?

T. J. SPONG:
Oh –

Your Grace, of course! We all had quite forgot!
Feel free, Your Grace, to say a word or two.

KING RICHARD:
My Grace? My Majesty, if you don't mind!

T. J. SPONG:
Your Majesty?

JANE TROUNCER:
Not yet!

T. J. SPONG:
Not till Act IV!

KING RICHARD:

It *is* Act IV.

WALTER WELKIN:
It *is* Act IV? Good God!

T. J. SPONG:

While we've been talking you have slaughtered on?
Drowned Clarence in the malmsey? Murdered Rivers?
Beheaded Hastings, Grey, and Vaughan? And then
The Princes in the Tower? And got the crown?

KING RICHARD:

I did it all as quietly as I could.
The audience, I'm certain, never noticed.

JANE TROUNCER:
Those poor young Princes smuggled to their deaths
Unfootnoted, unglossed, and unexplained?
In but one single version of the text?

WAYNE SCRUNGE:
And now you interrupt us once again?

KING RICHARD:
Just one familiar line, that's all I crave,
One last farewell, one final dying hint
Which play it was that we were playing here.

T. J. SPONG:
One single line we graciously concede.

KING RICHARD:
A horse! A horse! My kingdom for a horse!

WALTER WELKIN:
But some of us prefer the Second Quarto:
'I'm hoarse! I'm hoarse! I've shouted till I'm hoarse!'

JANE TROUNCER:
Oh, surely more authentic is the Third:
'A hearse! A hearse! I'm going to need a hearse!'

They fight. 'Richard III' is slain.

T. J. SPONG:
God and our notes be praised, victorious friends!
The day is ours; the bloody play is dead!

TWO READERS WRITE . . .

Darling, this book . . .

    – Which book?

This one.

    – You've finished it, have you?

Well . . . glanced through it. Got the general gist of it.

    – What's it about?

Oh, you know. This and that. The usual things. There's this couple in it, though, and they have these conversations, only you don't really know what they're talking about, and *they* don't know what they're talking about, and I just wondered if . . . well . . . if it's somehow supposed to be *us*.

    – Us? Why should it be us?

Well, this bit, for instance: 'Darling, this book . . .' 'You've finished it, have you?' 'Glanced through it. Got the general gist of it. There's this couple in it, though . . .'

– Oh no! The security services! We're being spied on!

How wonderful! After all these years! Someone actually listening to what I say!

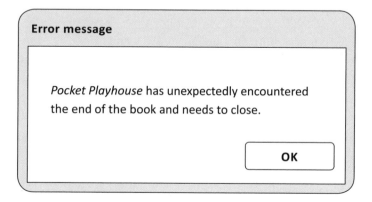

Error message

Pocket Playhouse has unexpectedly encountered
the end of the book and needs to close.

OK

Michael Frayn was born in London in 1933 and began his career as a journalist on the *Guardian* and the *Observer*. His novels include *Towards the End of the Morning*, *Headlong*, *Spies* and *Skios*. His seventeen plays range from *Noises Off*, recently chosen as one of the nation's three favourite plays, to *Copenhagen*, which won the 1998 *Evening Standard* Award for Best Play of the Year and the 2000 Tony Award for Best Play. He is married to the writer Claire Tomalin.